Please Return
Linda Hammerle
1811 Summerfield

Blue Collar Nomad

Also by Jake Kaida:

Bohemian Moss
Blue-Moon Epiphany
A Wandering Train to Now/The Revolution Starts Here
Dimestore Jargon

The following pieces included herein were originally published, unabridged or in excerpt form, under these or other titles, in literary journals and cultural magazines: *Understanding the Other Side of the Bar, Hot Springs, Upstairs at the Van Dyke, American Rhythm, Not another Literary Reference to Key West, Sweet Tamales at Christmas,* and *Wandering towards Autumn in Southern Oregon.*

For the Hammersla's,

It was a pleasure having a couple of Ohian's in my class. Your depth and humor added to its overall energy and enjoyment.

Blue Collar Nomad

The Literary Reflections of a Grassroots Pilgrim

By Jake Kaida

"Travel through Life"

J.K.

 Nomadic Devotion™ Books
Orlando, Florida

Bless your Path

Nomadic Devotion Books
Orlando, Florida

First Nomadic Devotion Books trade paperback edition: October 2014
Nomadic Devotion Books trade paperback ISBN: 978-0-692-28860-3

The Library of Congress has cataloged the Nomadic Devotion Books
trade paperback edition as follows:

      Kaida, Jake.
            Blue Collar Nomad / by Jake Kaida.

Library of Congress Control Number: 2014916266

ISBN: 978-0-692-28860-3

Printed in the United States of America
on recycled paper with plant-based inks
by 1984 Printing in Oakland, California.

A musical soundtrack for this book was composed by pianist Matthew Tavis Johnson. For information about or to purchase *Wandering: Blue Collar Nomad Soundtrack,* please visit www.nomadicdevotionbooks.com.

Dedication

I dedicate this book to those people and places throughout the United States and Canada that have sheltered and inspired me; and to the organic and spiritual wonder that emanates from the earth as well as those intuitive spheres that exist beyond conditioned thought.

I send special thanks out to the *Hearts of Space* radio show for supplying me with hundreds of hours of inspiration for my literary work and spiritual journeys over the years.

Finally, to Taquita, for your love and support of this project---helping it come to fruition in an authentic way.

Table of Contents

Foreword

This is a letter that was written to Jake Kaida at the beginning of his writing career by the late poet Joseph Langland. The wise and skilled Langland had a deep impact on Kaida at this greenhorn time in his life. It is included herein as both an honoring to a mentor and a prophetic salutation of a journey yet to come.

Dear Jake,

You are about one week away from your departure---knapsack and notebook in tow. I expect that you will come away from this trip having well-met yourself and the nature of things in foreign environments. With pleasure, of course.

As Robert Frost says in one of his classic little essays on poetry, "No tears in the writer, no tears in the reader." Meaning, of course, that "tears" can have many substitutes: laughter, pain, chills, sex, hunger, delight...well, you name it, and then pursue it. I have often said to myself: if I could have one great wish it would be to be able to invite John Keats out for a beer, or an evening, just after he had finished writing one of his great odes, say, "Autumn" or "Nightingale." All juices still flowing.

And to tell oneself to live richly and freely without throwing yourself away, and then getting some of it pinned down in words (elusive enough) for yourself, and others.

Our meeting? My privilege as well. Sharing a few hours? Mutual, of course. The immediate days ahead? Radiant, when the sensory apparatus is awake. Foreign places? Your "home" when you relate to it. Bon Voyage!

At the gate, on the dock, at the ramp, at the station, wherever, I would be glad to wish you well and send you on, as I do, of course. There are poems (and stories) ahead, awaiting your arrival.

Affectionately,

Joseph Langland

30 April 1998

Wandering re-establishes the original harmony
which once existed between man and the universe.

~Anatole France~

This collection of narratives, with some poems mingled within their bodies, is the literary expression of a period of my life, from late summer in 1998 when I had just turned twenty-three years old through autumn of 2010 when I was thirty-five years of age, during which I lived and worked nomadically. I had no set of directions for this journey, merely a youthful poetic enthusiasm that over time evolved into a grounded spiritual discipline.

During this era I rarely had more than a couple of hundred dollars in my savings account and sometimes held as little as five or ten dollars to my name. I also carried no handheld technological devices of any kind. If I needed to keep in touch with family or friends, I used a calling card at a pay phone or emailed them from a computer at a public library.

I slept in all manner of places, including: beaches, park benches, train stations, hostels, flophouses, tents, bridges, churches, tipis, retreat centers, monasteries, barns, farms, forests, lighthouses and parked cars. These lodgings were not always warm, dry or quiet, but more often than not did provide me with a place to write, reflect and rest.

I also became a connoisseur at eating remarkably well for under five dollars and finding spaces such as libraries, hotel lobbies, colleges, train stations, bookstores, supermarkets and tea shops to hang out in when it was cold or rainy. Maybe the most important part of these experiences is that they taught me to be truly thankful for each safe haven and life-giving meal, as I continually encountered and became the friend and acquaintance of many people who lacked basic food or shelter.

However, when I was wandering, moving from place to place for work or literary inspiration, I often found myself in settings that I had never been to before and where I had no acquaintances; this, coupled with nominal funds, often proved to be challenging and enlightening. Thus nomadicism is the greatest school that I have ever known.

During some of my more difficult times, my spirit needed to step up and inspire my mind and body to remind them that home is wholly within us. Thus migratory movement molded me into a holistically engaged person who adhered to (not some fundamental dogma or lofty ambiguous ethos) a grounded blue-collar philosophy that made me want to work with my hands and live close to the land. For I came to understand that it is through meaningful manual labor and service to others that we come into contact with the loving conscious aspect of our true self.

Eventually I had a go at a two year experiment where I bartered my labor for room and board and rarely had to use paper money. This undertaking led me to live and work at some out of the way places where I came into social communion with an ensemble cast of deeply caring unconventional human beings. Some of the more interesting ways that I was rewarded for my services during this time was with organic apples, farm fresh eggs, handmade paper, pumpkin pie, homemade wine, free-range chicken and a cozy tent next to a fruit orchard where I slept the sleep of angels.

Some of the agricultural labor that I took part in during my nomadic life included: picking grapes in upstate New York, harvesting apples and blueberries in British Columbia, Canada, designing culinary and meditation gardens along the central California coast, bucking firewood in Maine, collecting honey in the Hudson River Valley, helping out with various sustainable homesteads in

Oregon and Washington, planting trees and designing a found object landscape garden in Wyoming and creating an organic farm for a family on Cortes Island, Canada.

I have also worked at a fair amount of jobs in the hospitality industry, which includes but is not limited to dishwasher, bar-back, bartender, waiter, pizza-maker and cook throughout New Jersey, Maine, Ontario, Florida, Michigan, California, Texas, Wyoming, Oregon, Washington and British Columbia.

For if we are to move about the landscape, experiencing a variety of topographical regions and distinct social cultures, this movement should connect us deeply to the land we traverse and the people we meet along our way. It should also fine tune our intuition and deliver us towards our rightful work in this world.

Here I am going to say something about work, and what I believe work is. To me, every moment of our lives is work, a chance to connect with our natural environment, other human beings and our own deepest self; an opportunity to consciously evolve. A job is different from work. Billions of people in this world have been conditioned to believe that the definition of work is to have a job that you get paid for. But that is simply one kind of work. However it is the brand of work that most people desire and aspire to get.

The majority of my adult life has been spent doing another kind of work, participating in the development of grassroots connection and communication here on earth. I did not always get paid for this work, nor did I continuously seek material gain for my involvement, for the labor in itself is vital enough. This does not mean that I have not supported myself materially through jobs in the hospitality industry, as well as by farming, teaching and writing, because I have. But there have been long stretches during my adult life when I have given of my time and energy without thought of recompense. To be honest, it is those unalloyed interactions with human community, the earth, and universal spirit that sustain me rather than material prosperity.

All of the remarkable human beings that I have met during my nomadic life have been unadorned inborn individuals that would not succumb to the mindless societal death march: who realize their personal and universal responsibility to the world that we currently live in and co-create with one another. These great souls have taught me that we must live our innermost truth out into the greater world, no matter how difficult or uncomfortable it makes life for us or anyone else. Transformation does not occur in a vacuum and thus sometimes we must break many eggs in order to make an omelet that deeply nourishes creation.

To quote Ralph Waldo Emerson:

> "It is easy in the world to live after the world's opinion; it is easy in solitude to live after your own; but the great man is he who in the midst of the crowd keeps with perfect sweetness the independence of solitude."

It is important to note here that one who chooses an alternative route through life which eschews societal acceptance and weighs financial indulgence unimportant must understand that after a certain amount of time on your atypical journey it is impossible to ever go back to being a part of the society that you departed from. This is because your understanding of the interconnectedness of life, and maybe most practically, your work experience and resume, will make no sense to the average citizen or employer. Thus patience and perseverance will have to become living qualities in your being in order to be able to withstand the periods of time where you are offered no jobs or opportunities for kinship. That said there will always be hidden interior work to be done no matter what location or situation you find yourself in.

What sustains those of us who somehow discover and then listen to the still small voice within, letting it sustain and guide us through our unorthodox lives is the innate connection to something universally authentic and yet indefinable that burns inside us. We do not live for our own glory or personal comfort, but for that mysterious energy that binds everything together with love and wonder in true communion. This is not pie-in-the-sky idealism or a holier-than-thou ethics but the most down-to-earth perspective I have ever known. It is the perennial work and it requires and pays nothing but your true self.

During this period of my life nomadicism was my spiritual practice, and I adhered to that calling with verve and focus that allowed me to be present in a plethora of places with many different external and internal circumstances, which forced me to *die* to certain aspects of myself that no longer served my conscious evolution. This ongoing expansion of the self is a process that we all must go through on our path of individuation towards wholeness.

I do not recommend this experiential path to the comfort-seeking materialist, an ungrounded artist, the mechanically religious, the undisciplined spiritual seeker or the cerebral academic. For journeying into either the wilderness of the human psyche or an unknown stretch of forest; the vast inner space of our souls or a diner in a small town where everyone turns and looks at you when you walk through the door because you are the only strange face in the joint, can be a solitary and daunting *place* for the wayfarer to dwell.

However, as a human being who wishes to speak to and engage with humanity on many different levels, I had to be willing to step into the fray, as Lord Krishna employed Arjuna in the Bhagavad Gita, and not be afraid to get my physical hands dirty and my mental conditionings blown away. The evolution of my life and literary work follows this biological and psychological inquiry, which has been both a humbling experience of personal distillation and a wonder-filled journey of grassroots convergence with like-minded persons.

Perhaps the greatest purpose of my nomadic life and its literary expression was to enable me to begin to recognize the egotistical enchantments that afflict so many of us somewhere along our voyages. Perhaps in living close to the land and owning so few things, as well as by participating in many less than desirable jobs, such as cleaning toilets, mopping floors, weeding muddy garden plots, pulling out thorny bramble, grouting tile, and washing some of the muckiest dishes known to man, life finally helped to scrub away some of that debilitating ego residue that sticks like an encumbering film around our unfeigned hearts.

Ultimately, the writings within this tome reflect my willingness to engage with and be edified by the diverse yet unified aspects of place and community. They are not simply collections of words but flawed distillations that point to an organically rhythmic way of being in this world, which is disappearing more and more as people rely on their familial, societal, political, religious and other institutional tamings, as well as the controlled passivity of technology and virtual reality over holistically engaged personal experience and conscious environmental connection.

The roots of all of these writings were planted on bar napkins, matchbooks, cardboard boxes, beer coasters and white lined pages. They all began with the physical act of a human hand guiding a material writing utensil to inscribe words onto a tangible recording surface. Everything entered within this book was harvested and then distilled by an actual person out in the living breathing world. These pieces are arranged in chronological order so that you can journey along with me as I develop my craft as a writer and grow as a human being.

But then again, it is not the writer, or even the writings that are of lasting value herein, but what they attempt, albeit imperfectly, to point towards.

Jake Kaida

May 7, 2012

Rubino's in San Francisco

Life wandered across the country
for one month,
on the eve of my return
I sit overlooking the bay,
just another day,
at a crossroads in my life,
the next road leads on
until one day I will
sit in another restaurant
watching the waves of
my life roll into the
beach, silent
always wondering which
way the wind blows
the tide tomorrow,

distance
        seating
tunes
        loosely
groove
        bounces
leisurely
        stalking
envelope
        consciousness
amidst
        spontaneous
traffic
        cells   TAX
        THANK YOU

ARC 36   back →

while your music
floating down to our hearts,
embraces the aloneness.

It is that texture,
the exact haplessness,
I love about the jazz pianist.

                Jake

by Gates

The man who tried to dishonor The Beat

Truman Capote,
must have been,
a level man,
who couldn't
catch

Yet, he denounced
the simple setting
of Jack's type,
proving
his straight vision
could see
no buddhafields
in the plains.

A blind piano man
touches love
to the black and white,
through a romantic feel
of space)
a heavy-set cat
waltzes bells
up and down
the bass,
trapping the hollowed wood
for alternate groove--
and the weariness
of open sleep;
livingly exhausting
in our eyes
and lives,
present in jazz--

The Jazz Lounge
(Upstairs at the Van Dyke)

It is
the repercussions
of jazz,
hollowing
lonely cognac air --
mellows the soul.

Melting candlelight,
cozy round tables
nudged together,
interior relativity,
sits and meanders
the ear.
→

To Gary Snyder

If there is nothing,
and the mountains
and rivers
are nothingless
visions
of awakened emptiness--

Then,
where does the snow,
at the tip of the world
go--
when it melts
away.

Understanding the Other Side of the Bar
(Daytona Beach, Florida)

A storm threatened the flat never-ending Florida horizon as my father and I drove down the A1A highway. Heat-lightning nipped at the menacing dark purple sky. The last drops of light and the first of rain began to bathe the coast.

We pulled into the parking lot of the minor league ballpark and stood outside the truck like a couple of Seminoles asking a higher power to hold onto the precipitation. We did not look at one another, only up to the sky for a sign as to whether the game would be played, or if our father-son baseball outing would be rained out. As if the Great Spirit had heard our prayers, the ominous energy of the atmosphere loosened, and evening clarity reigned over the damp green and brown diamond.

My father had called me early in the morning to ask if I wanted to go to the Daytona Cubs baseball game with him. I said yes without even thinking about it. In hindsight, this meant that I would have to give up my Friday night bartending shift at the club I managed in St. Augustine, drive an hour down the A1A coastal highway to my parents' house in Palm Coast, and then drive another half hour from there over to Daytona with my dad. It would also mean that I would be surrendering to other less experienced hands the two or three hundred dollars in tips that I would make at the club that night. But I considered that money to be chump change compared to a chance to reconnect with my father.

I had moved down to St. Augustine, Florida, to finish up my undergraduate degree a couple of years before my parents had decided that they were going to retire from northern New Jersey to Palm Coast. Now that they were living about an hour south of me, I drove down and had dinner with them once or twice a month.

My father, who was a retired North Jersey police chief, had issues with my long hair, radical political views, lackadaisical attitude towards school, and deep affinities for Indian spirituality and meditation. However, I also knew that if there was one thing that could bring us together, it was baseball.

When I was little my dad used to take me to watch the Chicago Cubs play the New York Mets at Shea Stadium in Queens on my birthday. It just so happened that the Cubs, who were my favorite baseball team when I was young— even though the Mets and Yankees were our home teams—always played the Mets at Shea around the end of July. I still have a collection of programs and autographs from those games stored in a Cubs duffel bag in my closet.

My dad had also coached me in Little League when I was a kid, and was by far the best coach that I ever played for. By the time I got into high school I had. given up baseball to concentrate solely on getting a basketball scholarship to college. But I hadn't minded giving up what used to be my favorite sport, because the baseball coaches at my high school were nothing more than immature overgrown jocks who had never evolved enough to understand that coaching kids involves giving of oneself and not just belittling them and showing off to stroke your own aging ego. My father understood these things, and always taught his players not only the fundamentals, but also a love for the game, thus getting the best effort out of all of us.

As always, when I showed up at my parents' house to meet my dad so we could ride over to the ballpark together, he made some comment like, "When are you going to go back to wearing a crew cut?" Of course I had not worn a crew cut since I had played Little League baseball, but that fact never really seemed to settle into his consciousness. My mother would always just smile at me when my father made such remarks, and to break the tension reply, "He looks like Jesus."

As we walked into the small stadium, my father told me to go and pick us a seat while he went and got us something to eat. I strode up the bleachers to the last row that was covered by an awning but was open in front, presenting a perfect view of the glowing moon.

My father came back with hot dogs, pretzels, beer, and peanuts: the ballpark kind that are salted and roasted in their shells. We watched the game in silence---because he is my father and I am his son. We held our thoughts to a minimum, except for a few comments like: "good pitch," "go for two," and "he was safe," for the same reason.

After the game we walked back to the truck through humid night air. The kind of air only north Florida has: tranquil, heavy, and electric. As we neared his truck, my father tossed me the keys and said, "You drive." I unlocked the driver's side door, stepped up into the truck and placed the keys in the ignition.

I love driving my father's truck. I feel like I am more connected to him when I am pressing on his gas pedal or turning his steering wheel. It's like, if he has done it, and I am doing it, then maybe in some unspoken way that brings me closer to him. It brings him closer to me.

We drove over the bridge into Daytona Beach and got caught at a traffic light across the street from a strip of nightclubs and go-go bars. I turned on the radio to find some music to drown out the drunken yells of sunburned college kids and rednecks. After a few hip-hop and pop stations, I found Dylan, or, Dylan found us.

The light turned green, and my father and I started cruising along the famous Daytona strip. I turned up the music and began to sing. To my surprise, my father turned it up even louder. His voice met mine, a thousand miles below New Jersey on a crowded southern beach road, somewhere inside of our forgotten bond.

"How does it feel," we sang, as we started to see past the trivia and straight into the question: "What makes a man?" While Dylan spoke to us at this intersection of our lives, me twenty-four and my father fifty-something—the traffic light up ahead turned yellow and I caught his spirit begin to push up through the crust of his father's tough love, his mother's alcoholism, and twenty-five years of being a cop in North Jersey, and there were no words spoken, because with us there really never have been, and in this surge of family passion I pressed the gas pedal to the floor and we ripped through the amber light and all of those years of boys, men, fathers, sons, and their silence.

The acceleration of the truck and the wind rushing in through the open windows blew my long blonde hair and messed up the few black strands left on top of his head. I looked over at him and began to picture my father as a young man, strong and proud, a bull roaming his vast and fertile field. And even though that young man had chosen a direction and followed it to the end, he was now in a different place where no one knew he had worn that badge.

The cleansing light of the moon, which was perched above the rolling waves of the Atlantic, flowed through the passenger side window and washed over his aged skin. My father turned and looked out into the midnight blue sea for a long while. When the song eventually ended, he turned the volume down and then turned to me and said very clearly so that I would be sure to hear him, "I don't want to die here."

I looked over at him and asked, "Is your diabetes getting worse?"

"No," he replied. "It's got nothing to do with that. I just don't feel right down here. I don't belong here. I was the chief up there and everybody knew me. Down here I'm nobody. I miss New Jersey. I told your mother the other day that I want to go home."

"What did she say?" I asked.

"She said that she could only take so much tennis and golf," he replied with a smile. "We grew up on the same block up there, for Christ's sake. New Jersey is where we're from. It's who we are. And we are going to go back as soon as we can sell this house."

On the way back to my parents' transient home, my father and I stopped for a beer. I do not remember the name of the joint or what brand of beer we drank, but I do remember feeling that on that particular night it was nice to be on the other side of the bar. In between conversations with my dad I would watch the bartender. He was in his late forties or early fifties. He was tall and lean with deeply tanned skin, a few tattoos, and a long blonde ponytail. He served patrons with a sense of ease, and when he spoke, people listened. He seemed to be *in place*.

I dropped my father off well after midnight, got into my car, and cruised along the desolate but beautiful A1A coastal highway towards the quaint little beach shack that I called home. I loved living in St. Augustine. It was the first place that had made me look within myself to find out who I really was. Even though I only had a few weeks left before I graduated, and then was leaving on a long trip to Europe, for now I was content with where I was.

North Florida was the place where the son of a North Jersey cop had come to know himself as a bartender, a writer, and a spiritual being. It was the place where I let go of the city kid I had been and embraced all of the intimate changes that were occurring within me. But for my father, North Florida was the place where he built his dream house and retired to it, only to realize that home was something that he couldn't take with him. Home for him was a place that he knew and it knew him. This time in Florida was a jolt to his Taurus nature, and he was ready to leave.

As I drove, I remembered that my father and I had both played in the same Little League baseball system: him during the 1950's and me in the 1980's. Our home ballpark was named Nedellec Field. He grew up two blocks from it when he was a kid, and our house while I was growing up was a mere seven blocks away. During his final season of Little League, my dad played catcher, and had been crowned the town's "Home Run Champ." My last year, I had won the batting title by beating out strategically-placed bunts and spraying singles and doubles all over the field. I was also our town's best pitcher.

Looking back, it is interesting to see just how much our Little League baseball playing styles revealed about our lives now. My father had come to his triumphs through brute raw power, while I retired batter after batter by constantly changing my throwing motions and inventing new wind-ups. He belted the cowhide over the fence and onto the cracked macadam of the Smith School parking lot, while the hitters that I faced became entranced by my eccentric antics.

Maybe it was my unconventional Little League skills that eventually led me to embrace the karmic ever-changing nature of Indian spirituality with their thousands of odd deities. And maybe my openness to living in various places and embracing the evolutionary changes that occur within my psyche during my time there is why I am able to appreciate in a very unattached way where I come from, as well as where I live now.

But my father was raised Roman Catholic, and he has a hard time letting things go. He was born in North Jersey and he wants to die there. That's where his story is set.

Hot Springs
(Hot Springs, Arkansas)

I saw a sign that read, "Hot Springs, Arkansas, Hometown of President Bill Clinton." The light was fading away from the valley and the Ozark air was chilly. I rolled up my driver's side window, parked along a desolate side street, and walked over to a coffee shop to grab something warm to drink and a bite to eat. The cold air felt oddly consoling as it worked its way between the buttons of my flannel shirt.

The place was named "Wazzelle's." It was decorated with wood carvings of wizards and fairies, giving it a mystical vibe, a cross between a new age monastery and a mountain lodge. I ordered a mug of black cherry tea and a poppy seed muffin, and then wandered around the intimate space admiring the woodwork. A man with a handlebar mustache and a colorful Indonesian-style shirt came up and introduced himself.

"I'm Wazzelle," the man said.

"Jake," I answered and shook his hand.

"Just passing through?" he asked.

"Yeah," I answered.

"On your way to anywhere in particular?"

"Not really," I replied. "Just roaming around the country."

"And you just happened to roam into my coffee shop for some tea and a muffin?" Wazzelle asked.

"Looks that way," I responded.

"Ain't life funny like that?" he pondered.

"It sure is," I added. "Is this your work?"

"Yes it is. I've been carving since I was a child," Wazzelle explained.

"I like it a lot. These pieces must take you a lot of time," I stated.

"Time. Each piece takes as long as it takes. Time is simply a passing fancy we all die to relate to," he replied.

"I guess," I said.

"You don't go roaming all over the country just guessing about time," Wazzelle responded. "You take the time to do what you're doing, because there's no time to waste."

"Maybe," I replied.

"The wise man always plays the fool."

"Unless he really is one," I remarked.

"Stay a while and enjoy the music," Wazzelle said, before he walked back behind the counter to take another order.

A band had taken the small platform wooden stage in the back corner of the room, and to my surprise, during the brief bit of time that I had spent talking with Wazzelle, the room had filled up with an interesting crowd. The patrons were an eclectic mix of older New Age seekers in long colorful flowing dresses and chemises and younger and tougher pierced and tattooed artists. It felt more like a funky underground café in Budapest, not some hillbilly coffee shop along the main drag of Bill Clinton's hometown.

I found a small empty table in the back of the room, where I sat down with my tea and muffin. The band was playing a Neal Young song off of the album, "Harvest Moon." The singer was an older gentleman with a long white beard who looked like Gandalf the Grey from the Lord of the Rings. The rest of the band was much more youthful, and exhibited the stereotypical look of a punk band. They all had some kind of facial piercing and tattoos of tribal suns on their forearms. However, after listening to them jam for a while, it was apparent that they were all skillful musicians.

Out of nowhere, I heard a harmonica. I couldn't see the person playing it, but the sound was soulful, religious.

Then a black man came into my view as he limped over to the stage. He seemed like an abstract painting that had come into corporeality. I felt like I was starting to lose my mind, or perhaps gaining some higher form of consciousness the longer I sat in the room. Whatever this feeling was, whatever was happening to me inside this space, I never once thought of leaving but longed to be saturated by it even more.

The black man with the limp sat in with the band for a few songs, and then hobbled off the stage and sat down at the table next to mine. I couldn't help looking over at him, and as I turned my head in his direction, his eyes met mine. We had connected like Annie Dillard and that weasel in her short story. He got up, limped over to me, and asked "You wanna hear something I wrote earlier tonight?"

"Okay."

"Let's go outside then," he suggested.

He pushed open the glass door and the chilly valley night air washed over my now warm body. Even though he had a gimpy leg, he walked quickly as I followed him into a dark maze of side streets and narrow alleys. He had taken me away from Wazzelle's, away from the security and geniality of the other patrons and band, and was leading me into what seemed like a spiritual labyrinth.

"Got kicked by a horse when I was a kid," he said.

"What?"

"That's why I got this fucked up leg. I done got kicked by a horse when I was a kid," he restated. "You were wonderin why I got this limp?"

"I guess."

"You shouldn't go guessin if you know something to be true," he stated.

"Yes, I was wondering about your limp."

"I was raised on a farm right here in Hot Springs, and I ain't the smartest guy in the world. I've always been a little slow. They say I ain't got all my marbles. But ever since I was a kid I was always good with animals. I just had a way with them. One day though, this horse went nuts when I went out to take him for a ride. He went and kicked me right in the knee, and I never been the same," he explained.

"Did you go to a doctor?" I asked.

"My momma called the doc and he said he couldn't do nothin," he answered. "No matter, I get around just fine. I just don't look all pretty doin it that's all."

"Yeah, but if they could have helped you walk better, then they should have," I declared.

"The doc said there was nothin he could do and that's that. Ain't no sense in getting' all hot and bothered bout somethin happened over thirty years ago, especially when I wrote this here song earlier. Now let me play it for ya."

I sat down on the ground in a slender alley that framed the moon better than a pair of bifocals. Hard cold crept in through my threadbare denim. He started to play. I sensed his love for the instrument, for the sound it professed to the world, for our shared space in the alley and for every star in the sky. He was full of love, full of sound. He played music for everything, not for an audience, not for me, I was merely the invitation his soul needed to become public. He had invited me out, so that I would invite him in. One other person truly listening to him was all he needed to become totally unleashed. He was lost inside of universal rhythm, and I got found watching him.

The next morning, I met Tony at a park in the center of downtown. This became my favorite place in Hot Springs. There was a huge grass lawn with lots of flowers, wooden benches, and two pools of thermal spring water. That healing water was what Hot Springs was famous for. Bath House Row, a collection of old bathhouses, some of which were still in service, stood prestigiously along the historic downtown thoroughfare as history markers of Hot Springs' passed association with high class American society. Theodore Roosevelt and Al Capone had both bathed in the waters of "The Peaceful Valley" as its residents referred to Hot Springs.

But my harmonica playing friend wasn't taking me to bathe in Hot Spring water. He was taking me to, "My favorite spots. You gotta remember, I grew up here. I know all the secret spots. The spots the tourists don't know 'bout. I'll show you the real beauty. It's all back in the mountains."

We set off through downtown and wound up on a trail that led up into Hot Springs National Forest. We walked and talked for well over an hour, before arriving at a lake. The water was a dark, murky blue and was surrounded by a ring of trees along the shoreline. A rickety wooden bridge was the lone way to cross the water. As we made our way along the bridge, Tony asked me to stop so he could play me a song.

I sat down cross-legged and placed the fingertips of my right hand in the cool Arkansas H2O. While the tiny ripples upon the surface of the lake tickled my fingertips, I watched him melt into that wondrous rhythmic world he had brought me to the night before. In the daylight, it proved even easier to let myself go. Everything around me was alive and lighted with mystical charm. After a few minutes, he said, "Chime on in. Come on, gimme some words."

I began to sing out exactly how I felt at that moment. His music in that place had overwhelmed my spirit, opening up a floodgate to a clear uninhibited space of language. I don't know exactly what was said, but I knew it was real, and I surrendered to it. Tony seemed real happy with my lyrics too, because his harmonica playing got even hotter.

Certain Native American tribes have a belief in "The Trickster." Tony was not a Trickster, but if all one garnered of him was his Southern sticks enunciation and his gimpy gait, and let that stop them from inviting him into their life so that he could saturate their soul with the music of place, then they had been duped by the material universe.

After we hit a crescendo, I felt like it was a good time to stop. I had hit my stride, sent my message out into the world and there was no need to over play it. Tony felt my intention and finished off our spontaneous piece with a descending solo that channeled us softly back into our bodies. Then, he limped over, extended his hand, helped me to my feet and guided me further into the glistening backwoods.

Scenes: From a Summer in Gainesville
(Gainesville, Florida)

1

Sometimes the darkness knows where to find the light, or at least show you if there is any. Gainesville's kind of like that. I came here on a leap of faith, and already I hear the humming of the drums when your faith turns into grace. I've only been here a few days, but this town has one of those vibes that envelopes you. It's a southern college town where everyone's a transient except for the locals and the transients who forgot to leave. I've been a transient for so long that I'm kind of happy to be settling somewhere for a little while.

A lot of people ask me why I moved to Gainesville. I tell them because it's cheap to live here and I love the sky. At dusk I view the most beautiful pink, purple and blue hues. The only sky that is comparable to North Central Florida is in the Cyclades, a group of Greek islands sitting in the Aegean Sea, and also some places in New Mexico and Arizona. But aside from those locations you're hard pressed to find such enchanting sunsets.

The first time I drove to Gainesville I watched a lightning storm appear and disappear within twenty minutes. I was crossing the bridge over from Palatka when three jagged bolts blasted the pastel horizon.

I don't like South Florida because it's all palm trees, saggy tans, breast implants and northern transplants. Gainesville though, this is the real South: crazy college football fans, good barbecue, lots of secondhand stores and little liquor sheds; and the vegetation is lush: hanging Spanish moss, huge palmettos, vibrant flowers and even a cactus mixed in occasionally.

Life, it's slow here. The air is thick as a gator's skin. When you step outside in the morning it seeps into your pores, which open up like the tear ducts on an inspired gospel singer. The sweat is fresh. It lets you know the days are long. People stroll down the street. They feel the humidity and allow themselves more time because of it.   These people aren't *tres chic* like Parisians or cosmopolitan like New Yorkers, but they know who they are and where they're not going and I like that.

2

I go for a bike ride every night around dusk. I feel like a ghost when I pedal through the narrow tree covered side streets and wonder if the people I pass can see me, or if they merely sense a golden blur. Somebody once told me that dawn and dusk are the most energizing times of the day; the best times to wander into the vibes of different dimensions. At dusk, the leaving light grows most intense before it's gone so the trees and grass seem greener, more alive.   The whole earth breathes in an elevated state.

I like to coast up people's walkways at night while they are watching TV. It freaks them out to see a stranger staring inside their window, but I want to see what their world is like. But like all people who sit and die in their houses, they're just passing the time.

3

I made my first friend down here. A girl named Robyn. She's twenty-nine and doesn't look or act a day over nineteen. Last night she called and told me that she was coming to pick me up to go look at a desk. I needed a desk to put my word processor on. Robyn honked the horn and when I walked outside, she was sitting in the driver's seat of a black Crown Victoria macked-out to look like an undercover police car, complete with tinted windows, spotlight and CB radio.

Robyn told me that she likes to pull up real fast behind other cars and watch them slow down. Then, she said, "They keep checkin their rearview to see if I'm still there." She said she actually got pulled over in a cemetery one night for impersonating a police officer.

The desk was out on her front porch but was only high enough for a small child. I asked her how I was supposed to fit my legs under it and she replied, "Hey man, you wanted a desk. This is a desk. I can't help it if you're daddy-long-legs."

Inside her house, Robyn had a bunch of Buddhist tapestries hung on the walls and a Ted Nugent album on top of her record player. She has a dog, Austin, whom she says found her, and two cats. All of her pets have fleas, but she won't dip them because of her Buddhist beliefs. Robyn says, "Fleas are beings too."

"But they're feasting on your pets," I replied.

"I do comb them if it gets too bad," she said. "But to give them (the fleas) a chance, I take them off the comb, put them in my hair and run into the shower."

"Why the hell do you do that?" I questioned.

"Because then they get a chance to swim down the drain and find their way back out into the world," she answered.

I sat there for a few moments and then yelled questioningly, "You put fleas in your hair?"

"I guess that's one of those things you don't really say out loud," she replied.

We sat and talked for a while longer and then she gave me a ride home. In the car, Robyn told me that she's lived in Gainesville for eight years and knows the side roads like the back of her hand. "You see," she says, "Gainesville runs on a grid. Everything is NE, NW, SE or SW something."

4

It rains every day between four and five o'clock in the late afternoon here in Gainesville during the summer.

The rain cools the place down and breaks up the monotony of light and dark. I think I take after my dad. He used to sit on our front porch in the Northeast and watch the thunderstorms. Now I understand why. Thunderstorms are
cleansing. It's like the creator washes the whole smelly world with them.

5

It's been a few slow, sticky, hot Southern days. Nothing but bike rides, working out, listening to music and writing. The amazing thing about Gainesville is if you pedal a couple of blocks in any direction from the university, it's like you're in a whole different time zone. It's not the old South, more like the forgotten South. Streets are covered over by sweeping Magnolia trees and Spanish moss awnings that shade the poor folk from the heat.

The poor folk, who are almost entirely black, with a few old white hippies and anarchistic white youth thrown in the mix, sit out on their falling apart front porches humming songs or knitting or drinking whiskey from the bottle while playing cards with lots of old tires, weathered row boats and rusted gardening tools strewn about their front yards.

Every third block or so has a small ad hock community garden where they grow collard greens, summer squash and tomatoes. I like pedaling around back there because I don't feel as detectable as I do downtown or by the university. I feel more like a convivial wandering ghost, swerving and sweating in the midday squalor of the Gainesville sun.

6

I respect the hard-working, blue-collar black folk down here in Gainesville. I see them hanging out at the LIL' Champ or ABC liquor store trying to soak up some life and catch a little buzz before their break is done and they have to go back to working for the man. And the man can't understand what it is they feel during these breaks or why it carries their tired backs through the rest of the day. Well let me tell you "man," these folks got soul plain and simple. You can't teach soul, it's something that seeps into you, like the vitamins from the pot liquor at the bottom of a bowl of collard greens.

7

I was playing tennis by myself earlier; hitting a furry green ball against a brick wall over and over again. It was over a hundred degrees out, and although I was sweating profusely, the game kept my attention off how hot it actually was. It's so hot down here that if you don't keep your mind occupied with something, it instantly slips into heat depression.

I was starting to swing into a good groove when one of the strings on my racket broke. It's times like these when I question the existence of a benevolent force in the universe. Why couldn't that "great power" hold the damn string together? I was finally starting to hit good. My mind wasn't constantly belly-aching about the heat, and a pretty blonde girl had started hitting a ball against the wall next to me.

But with a string down and no real desire to play handball, I decided there was only one thing for me to do to salvage any hope of happiness from the afternoon. So I sat down on the grass and watched the sweat pour down every collegiate inch of her tanned and toned body.

8

It's been a few tough days. Thank God the sun is going down. In the darkness, the world is much more bearable to the lonely soul. It gets a little bit cooler here too. It must have been 100 degrees with full humidity in Gainesville the last couple of days. All that heat and perspiration makes the time go by real slow. I'd have to say that right now, I'm lonely. I'm not sad or depressed or anything like that; I just don't know many people here.

At the moment, it's a little bit after eight o'clock on Friday night and the college students are either stumbling around drunk from happy hour or pre-partying inside of their apartments before going out later. I am sitting on a lawn chair out on the concrete slab terrace of my apartment watching the fading light of another Gainesville summer day slip into a vast purple firmament.

It's time like this when one realizes that the only way to experience loneliness is alone. The crazy thing is that there are thousands of college students going to summer school, but I don't think any of them can see me. I'm not sure if I come into their line of vision, or if I do, maybe they don't care enough about someone outside of their world to try to let them in.

But the humble black folk sure know I'm here. Like the other day, when I was biking home from the gym in the blinding heat of the midday sun, this middle-aged black man on an old beat-up children's bike was pedaling up a hill while I was cruising down the opposite side. That man, amidst all of his sweat and tortured expressions with his knees hitting against his chin, managed to look across the road and shoot me a big old smile and a nod while I did the same right back at him. It was as if he was saying, "Don't worry about them spoiled college kids. It's all about developing your soul. And hey, we each got these cool bikes so it can't be that bad right?"

9

I started working as a bartender in a brewpub downtown. The owners are eccentric, but not in a good way, more of a weird unsociable way. I'm not crazy about the clientele either. The customers are either the owners' annoying beer club buddies or members of the University of Florida's many fraternities and sororities. Either way, I'm dealing with people who want to get as drunk as possible and do not tip accordingly.

The thing I like about the job is that I've met some cool people. Two in particular: Dave, a fellow electronic music fan, who, it turns out, grew up a couple of towns away from me, and Stephanie, a pretty, friendly, wryly funny twenty year old who loves Depeche Mode and The Cure. In fact, the first time she gave me a ride home from work, she had my favorite song, "Just Like Heaven," cued up on her CD player.

10

I went to Poe Springs with Stephanie today. It is one of a cluster of natural springs that Alachua County has hidden deep within its pastoral land. We listened to Depeche Mode and The Pixies as we wound through the rural routes of North Central Florida, passing cow pastures, roadside vegetable stands and shotgun shacks with confederate flags nailed to their sides.

When we arrived at the entrance gate, we kidded around with the woman collecting the money that we had

to go to Poe Springs because we were both "so po'." To
get to the springs, we wandered down a narrow wooden
boardwalk through swamps and still pools covered over
by thick green algae. The water of the springs remains a
constant 72 degrees year round, which is very soothing
when one is always sweating and sluggish from humid
hundred degree weather.

The attribute that I remember most about the springs
goes perfectly with what Stephanie said to me when we
first got out of the water to go and lay in the sun. She
said, "It doesn't even feel like water, but more like a
holistic gel that skims over your body." I remember
thinking that was exactly it, as I lay on the grass feeling
purified and cooler than I had at any other time during the
summer.

11

It's a little past nine o'clock at night, and I'm sitting on
the grass of the Gainesville Downtown Community Plaza
listening to a blues guitarist strum songs about the
Southland. It is late August and the sun is setting.
Remnants of the fading burn leave the North Florida
horizon spray-painted with pink, purple and orange tags
of leftover heat.

It occurs to me, as I look around this lawn, that this is
the way life should be: families, children, friends and
lovers strewn about the grass on blankets, listening to
music, staring up at the stars, dreaming and living under
one cosmic rooftop. There is no color or class at times like
this, only rhythm and community. Music, over the years,
has done more to bring people together than I think any
of us really know. When we are lost inside of rhythm, our
communal, tribal, ritualistic instincts return to carry us
inside of ourselves to a purer abode, a habitation without

judgment or the necessity for money: a vibrational harmonious place where we co-exist within the music.

The South may have the most communal rhythm of any region in the United States. Whites and blacks have lived here together longer than anywhere else in this country, and although there is still ignorance and prejudice among some, there is also an understanding, a deep soil of community that has developed between the people, no matter what color. Inside of the heat and sweat of these slow Southern days, I am beginning to feel, starting to fathom, the fecundity of that dirt.

Staring Chloe
(Athens, Georgia)

Late Thursday night or early Friday morning

It was 4:34 a.m. and I was sitting in a booth at a 24 hour diner in the heart of downtown Athens. The tall silver container that once held chocolate malt painted sweat collages onto the table in front of me. The ceiling fans spun smoky air, pasting patrons in greasy funk. A neon pink jukebox played "Six underground" by the Sneaker Pimps, while a pot belly drag queen hiked up his dress and danced on the table next to me. A waitress with a safety pin stuck through her lip walked by carrying a platter of burgers and fries. The small flipping chalkboard showed off the daily specials. A glowing white sign in the back read "EATS."

I had nowhere to sleep. Maybe, in the morning, I would drive outside of the city and rest in a field. Now, I watched the night throw up on itself.

Friday night

I was sitting on a bench downtown with a slight buzz on, watching the light become dark, but not darkness. My sight was still easily seen. Everyone I saw was either walking or seated. I was traveling. This night had its own sound: whispers, hollers, loud-talkers, silent head-down walkers, and college students slurping cappuccinos. Fall was beginning to tap into Georgia. Florida was still hot and humid, but up here, in a tank top, my skin was tight.

Saturday night

Outside of a coffee shop I watched her walk by me. After she passed, she turned and stared. Then she went inside and came out a few minutes later with a tall steaming cup. She walked by me again, and when she was about 20 yards away, stopped, looked back and stared.

About 10 minutes later, I felt a presence passing behind my body. Then, it moved in front of me, stopped, stared and spoke, "I'm Chloe," the girl said.

"Jake."

"You don't live here."

"Nope."

"Why are you here?" she asked.

"My friend and I DJ'd at the One Love Music Hall last night."

"So, you're a DJ?" she inquired.

"No, I'm a poet. But I love music so I spin for cash," I answered.

"No shit. I'm a poet."

"Figures," I said.

"I know," she responded.

"You've got a pretty cool town here."

"Yeah," she replied, "but once you live here, its like a magnet. Athens has some strange hypnotic power. It won't let you leave, I've tried."

"Where'd you go?" I asked.

"I drove cross country and landed out in Salem, Oregon."

"Did you like it out there?"

"It was good for a while, but I had to leave because it rained too much," she stated. "Hey, do you want to go on top of that building over there? It's the highest point in Athens. You can see the whole valley from up there."

"Sure," I said.

We ran up countless flights of stairs, stopping only once to catch our breath and laugh. The view at the top was an organic TV set glowing in the empty night: street lights and wires, mountains and blackness were all we could see for miles.

After descending to downtown reality, Chloe bummed us a ride back to her house, which was in the country about twenty minutes outside of town. As we pulled onto her grassy driveway, I started seeing the lyrics to the R.E.M. song, "It's the End of the World as We Know It," spelled in the stars.

We walked into her house where I was introduced to her father, who was lying on the floor listening to a jazz album on an old record player. We started talking about jazz, and then he walked over to a wooden cabinet and took out a tape. He handed the tape to me, *Giant Steps* by John Coltrane, and said, "Keep this with you at all times. It just makes sense."

Chloe went into the kitchen and came back with an open bottle of wine. She then escorted me out the screened door and into the back yard. We walked together through pitch black forest darkness to her small shack in the woods. It had been her father's tool shed, but when Chloe came back from Oregon, after her soul had been sickened by all the rain, he helped her convert it into a cozy artist's den.

Chloe opened the door, walked inside and lit a candle. Then she took my hand and guided me into her space. It was powerful. A woman's energy in the woods. Chloe was a poetess. A nymph. She was fire in the darkness. I felt her words all around me.

She grabbed the guitar and sat down on a little stool next to the bed. I lay down as she began strumming. She started singing, discoursing with the night. Chloe was speaking to me, in a voice so direct; I feared we would never climb back out of that oblivion. A strong wind slipped through the open window and extinguished the candle. Chloe put her guitar down, pressed play on the stereo and climbed onto the bed next to me. I opened my arms. She slithered in. I held her. We listened to our space:

> *There are so many eternities that we forget in togetherness. We have no rules, forms, or words when we are making our poems. However, years from now, I may be alone, standing, looking out towards some far-away cliff, and thinking of you, the drop, the valley between myself and that other land, may melt, or, it may seem as if my whole world waited for you, and then, like all dreamers, when you tapped me, I couldn't wake up to truly understand what daydreams hold.*

Monday

We woke early in the afternoon. Chloe borrowed her brother's car and drove me into the downtown, where I was supposed to catch a ride back to Gainesville with my friend. She dropped me off at the corner by the diner. She stayed in the car. She didn't say goodbye. She didn't say anything. It would end how it all started. She just sat there and stared at me, like she knew me, or had known me. I sat on a bench and watched.

Happy Thanksgiving (in Street Prose)
Ottawa, Canada

I'm writing in this coffee shop
down in the Glebe
which is the trendy section of Ottawa
when one of the guys working
asks me if I want a sandwich
because they're going to throw the leftovers away
there's about eight of them sitting there
so I grab a turkey
and head out to my bike
just as I unlock my bike
I get this idea
to feed some homeless people
with the rest of those sandwiches
so I go back to the door
but it's already locked
so I start riding home
but now I'm inspired
my idealism is in overdrive
so I say to myself
I'll give away my sandwich
because hey it was free anyway
but that's not enough
I start pedaling faster
when I realize
I have a fresh loaf of bread at home
I'll make peanut butter and jelly sandwiches
did I mention it's Thanksgiving
I get home around 11:30 P.M.
and make three peanut butter and jelly sandwiches
wrap them each in tin foil
take them along with the turkey
and throw them in my backpack
but I don't feel that's enough

so I make one more
five sandwiches
and I feel good
I ride down Elgin
and pass the spot
where I always see
this one guy and his dog
but they're not there
I go up to Bank
which usually has some homeless
but nothing
it's now around midnight
so I say to myself
pedal downtown by the Market
the bars should be busy
and there's probably some homeless
hanging around there
trying to bum some change
I get there
and I don't see anyone
but girls dressed in tight pants
and little tops
and buff guys walking around
with their cold nipples
showing through spandex shirts
then I see
a pretty Hispanic prostitute
standing on the corner
but she probably doesn't want a sandwich
I pedal around for a little longer
now it's past midnight
and I'm pretty cold on my bike
but I'm still industrious
buzzing with the adrenaline

heaven sends it workers
I can feed the homeless
five to be exact
and dammit I'm going to
I pedal around a little more
but there's just lots of drunk kids
yelling and hooking up
then I ride past these three guys
and they say
hey buddy can you spare a joint
I say sorry got nothing and keep pedaling
but I turn around
ride up to them
and ask them if they're hungry
they say yes
I say well since its Thanksgiving and all
I've got some sandwiches for you
the one guy says turkey
I say I've got one turkey
and the rest peanut butter and jelly
the one guy grabs the turkey
and the other guys go ahhh
I wanted that one
I hand the other guys
peanut butter and jelly
and the one guy goes
I'll save this for later
we just smoked some weed
and I don't want to kill my buzz
and I think okay whatever
they say god bless you brother
I say peace out
hold up two fingers and pedal away
I stop at a traffic light

and wonder if they are truly homeless
or just some stoned guys
jonesing for food
and then I think
what's the difference
it was a positive connection
and if they're not truly homeless
does that mean they don't deserve my bread
but when you're saving the world
you want to save the right ones
if you know what I mean
but who are the right ones
I probably need to be saved too
I'm just not hungry that's all
now I have two sandwiches left
so I ride back to Elgin
where this homeless woman
always sits on a blanket
with a hat in her hand
for monetary donations
she's probably the most recognizable
homeless person in Ottawa
a permanent fixture of vagrancy
spotting the nation's capital
I ask her if she's hungry
because I've got some sandwiches
she smiles at me
and says she doesn't take food from strangers
and I think
doesn't she know I'm an angel
I ask her why not
she smiles again
and says think about it
and I do think about it

and the only thing
I can come up with
is that maybe she thinks
someone will poison her
or maybe we already have
maybes she's seen me pedal by her
about thirty times since I moved here
maybe she knows
I poisoned her thirty times already
I bet she has good eyes
then I start thinking
if I and everyone else with a home
have lost our sight
what if I'm blind
I have two sandwiches left god dammit
and I can't see any homeless people
maybe they all found homes since yesterday
maybe I lost my sight in the dark
I'm probably pedaling right by them
I just can't see them
huddled in the dark
in the alleys
on steps and stoops
park benches
or just standing there
with bags in their hands
that's it I'm blind
then I actually do see a guy
who might be homeless
but he's flailing his arms around
and talking to himself
on the sidewalk
and I think
he might snap on me

so I don't offer him a sandwich
but maybe he already saw right through me
I bet he has great eyesight
now I'm getting desperate
how can I be a savior
if I can't find anyone to save
but a few dope heads with the munchies
I try Bank again
and then Elgin
but just more kids
at more bars
emptying out into more night
they're totally blind
at least I have some sight
but who am I kidding
I've got two sandwiches in my backpack
and I'm pedaling home
I'm like Gandhi without India
I start thinking
about why I couldn't find people to feed
and why my vision is so bad
and why people
keep getting blinder
and drunker
so I go home
and unwrap one of the sandwiches
P B and J
not as good as my mom used to make
but not bad for a partially blind man
I put the other sandwich
in the fridge
and tell myself
I'll try to give it
to someone tomorrow

during the day
when the light's better
Happy Thanksgiving.

Upstairs at the Van Dyke
(South Beach, Miami)

As I stepped off the long distance bus in Miami, the humid scent of Latin-American heat enveloped my senses. I had fifty dollars to my name and a reservation for a hostel on Washington Avenue. Instead of hailing a taxi, whose tourist meter would quickly drain my remaining funds, I boarded a local bus that wound through every slum and strip joint street in Miami, until I finally got off at a stop along a canal where I had to wait almost an hour in dank ninety degree heat for another bus.

After two buses, and close to two hours, I arrived at Washington Avenue with my shirt stuck to the rucksack on my back. I walked for a few minutes and then found my place, the Clay Street Hostel, located on a quaint side street. The lobby was a bustling social zone where I overheard many languages being spoken. After checking in, I went up to my room and found a young Korean guy asleep on one of the bottom bunks.

It was the middle of the day in the middle of November and the room was boiling hot. I could see sweat all over the Korean guy's sheets and T-shirt. So instead of attempting at what could only become a muggy, dismal nap, I decided to walk around and become more familiar with the new place I had arrived at. The first thing I noticed was that the hostel was located across the street from Madonna's nightclub, "Liquid." I also became aware of Washington Avenue's large homeless population. None of them hassled me for change though. I guess it was obvious I didn't have any, or perhaps they were all too tired and worn out from the heat to bother.

I quickly learned, from a local guy I had a conversation with at a smoothie bar, that Washington Avenue is considered to be the cracked-out distant cousin of glitzy Ocean Drive. Ocean Drive is the posh gathering place for models, fashion designers, photographers, actors and actresses, and everyone else from all over the world who wants to be seen by those people whose lives are watching and commenting on the scene.

Most days, as I would come to witness, hordes of people sat out at the scores of cafes packed along Ocean Drive, wearing their coolest outfits and dark sunglasses, hoping to be noticed or find someone worth noticing. It did not take me long to realize that the world of South Beach was just like the evening news show of any major U.S. city, constructed for our viewing pleasure. People came to South Beach to fantasize, to role play with reality. At the very least it was a pseudo-entertaining show. At its worst it could become an all-consuming bottomless pit of soullessness.

I had been living in Ontario, Canada, before the lure of working the season in sunny Miami had harangued my mind into dragging my body down to South Florida. My soul was never really into the decision to come, but my soul did know that it loves to travel, and after three months of living in Canada without a legal work permit my funds had been reduced to a bare minimum. This meant that I had to pick a place to live, work for a while, and stick it out until I could save enough money to leave.

It had already snowed five or six times by early November in the capital city where I lived up in Canuck-land, thus I picked South Beach for its emblematical warmth and palm trees. However, physical warmth does not always translate into a feeling of social, psychological, or spiritual warmth. Feelings of displacement aside, I had to find a job.

Work, when one finds himself in a place whose outer landscape is not exactly matching his inner topography, is a way for said individual to dive into a substrata within that larger foreign universe in order to satiate the soul long enough to make the process of being there and saving up some money bearable, and hopefully even a learning experience to build upon. So on my second day in the decadent Mecca of America, I hit the streets in my one pair of nice clothes, resume in hand, and searched for a bartending gig. I had not even walked a whole three blocks before I landed a one night engagement working as a barback for the opening party of a Latin jazz club on Washington Avenue.

As I needed to be at work by three o'clock that afternoon in order to help the bartenders set up, I walked straight back to the hostel where I showered and changed into black pants and a black button down shirt, grabbed some rice and beans at a little Cuban grocery store, and after eating my hearty meal sitting under the shade of a palm tree on the curb of an unheralded back street, headed over to the club to begin my work in the hospitality industry of South Beach.

That night I made a hundred bucks cash for grabbing cases of beer from the walk-in cooler and stocking the ice wells for the female bartenders, who were all career bartenders in their late thirties and early forties with too much make-up splashed all over their faces and tight miniskirts with skimpy tops showing off the soft flesh of their stomachs. These women were efficient bartenders who easily handled the swarms of patrons shouting out their drink orders, but to me also symbolized the inability of the South Beach psyche to come to grips with the natural aging process as something that adds character and refinement to the person, rather than being an organic saboteur that either needed to be run away from or blatantly denied.

Despite the heat and lack of air conditioning, I liked staying at the Clay Street Hostel. The place had an eclectic, international flavor: there was Alex, a fashionable young gay guy from Prague who loved mojitos; Richard, a well-built but a little too short aspiring model from Amsterdam; Heidi, a stunning blonde hair blue-eyed Kiwi (New Zealander), who every straight guy at the hostel lusted after and all the gay guys bitched about in private but latched onto in public; and finally, Cubby, one of my roommates, a short, stocky Korean kid who had moved to South Beach from Minnesota a week earlier.

It turned out that Cubby was running away from a bad relationship. Back in Minnesota he had found out that his girlfriend of the past four years had been sleeping with his best friend for the last three. If that was not bad enough, Cubby had spent all the money he had earned working in a fish-packing warehouse on their rent, food, and even bought her a used Honda Civic. To put it bluntly, Cubby got played. So he quit his job, cashed his last paycheck, and took the long, grueling Greyhound bus trip from Minneapolis to South Beach.

Cubby was a study of the effect that specific actions and their subsequent psychological damage have upon the notion of place. I could see how the mere mention of the word Minneapolis opened up a bleeding wound in his psyche, even more than when he talked about his girlfriend or his best friend and their lustful, traitorous acts together. This is because Minneapolis had been the first place he had moved to upon leaving his family's home in Chicago. It was his first place of independence and love. Thus he was now displaced from the only locale where he had ever known himself outside of his family unit and local community.

This sense of lost individual place deeply effected Cubby. For him, that bus trip from Minneapolis to South Beach provided the framework for psychological distance to begin so that the ultimate act of healing may eventually occur somewhere down the line. However, within the macrocosmic seasonal nature of South Beach and the microscopic transient nature of the hostel, Cubby was unable to set himself in place to begin that healing process. All his unresolved pent-up emotions could do were fester here in Miami.

Cubby and I became good friends, and I cherished the time we spent together, because the depth of his suffering at least lent the air we breathed together in South Beach a hint of soulfulness, providing me with a purpose beyond simply making enough money to get the hell out of Miami. He regarded me as some kind of spiritual older brother, and I think that I was the first person who he ever spoke with about what happened to him in Minnesota. Around the other guys at the hostel Cubby would always act the macho figure, commenting on various girls' asses and talking about how he was going to go out that night and get himself a bodacious Brazilian hottie', but as he spoke I always looked into his eyes, which betrayed any sense of lust for the opposite sex. I think what he wanted most of all was for any female to give him a long soulful hug and tell him that there would be another woman who would cherish him for who he was.

Eventually Cubby left on another Greyhound bus, this time from South Beach bound for Chicago. He needed a place that he knew and people that knew him within that place to truly begin to let go of what had happened to him. South Beach was where he ran to, and it did provide him with distance and a true friend, yet sometimes there is nothing like family and one's childhood home to comfort and soothe the soul with the nourishing balm of psychological and social familiarity with place.

As for me, after Cubby departed I realized that I had way too much time on my hands, as my only work was as a bartender for a high class catering firm that provided me with wonderful jobs working celebrity parties, but only a few times a week. Thus I became friends with Miguel, one of the owners of the café that was attached to the Clay Street Hostel. Miguel was also the head chef of the café, and previous to moving to South Beach had worked all over the world as a personal chef for extremely wealthy people. Miguel had tons of stories to tell about his eccentric clients and the exotic dishes that they would have him create. He told me that he had sailed around the world with an Australian millionaire who used to have Miguel make him homemade Belgian waffles topped with broiled shrimp and chocolate sauce every Tuesday night.

Miguel lived in one of the rooms of the hostel that had been converted into a rather small but plush studio in order to accommodate him. When he wasn't working he would sit outside on his veranda, which was shaded by an immense palm tree and looked out over the quaint side street. Whenever he saw me walking by he would call out, "Hola Jake, would you care for a cerveza?" I usually did, so I would walk up to his room, grab a Presidente from the fridge, and relax in the seat across from him.

I knew that Miguel was gay, and that he had a crush on me. Yet I also enjoyed his company and could see that he understood that I was heterosexual and that it was not in the realm of possibility for him to turn me to the other side. Besides, the air was cooler up there on his veranda, and those soothing tropical breezes combined with the alcohol and our talks about traveling the world made South Beach seem kind of human, and during its highly vivacious pastel sunsets, almost poetic at times.

One afternoon when I realized that I was not really saving any money and had been living in South Beach for over two months, I took a stroll down Lincoln Road, a highly trafficked pedestrian area with restaurants, perfume shops, and trendy high class clothing boutiques. I noticed the deep red Spanish style veneer of the "Van Dyke" immediately. It seemed like an intimate place full of stories and characters, somewhere that would allow my poetic sensibility to unfold within this materialistic sensory carnival.

I asked the hostess at the outdoor podium if they were hiring and she replied, "Go inside and take a seat. I'll go get Al for you." I sat down at a high round cocktail table that faced onto the outdoor pedestrian mall, and watched the fashionistas sashay up and down the quay. While I was sitting there, a guy with an iguana on his shoulder asked if I wanted my picture taken with Harry, the iguana, for five dollars. I told him no and petted the iguana on its back.

Al came over to the table and greeted me warmly. He was about 5'7 and very slight. He seemed wired, like maybe he was on something, as most restaurant and bar managers I had worked for over the years had been, but he was also very nice and after quickly glancing at my resume was very anxious to get me started working at the Van Dyke. He hired me on the spot.

The Van Dyke became my sanctuary from the rich and materialistic vibe that saturated South Beach almost as much as the dog poop that lay in small piles on the sidewalks. This was because when you think that your shit doesn't stink, you certainly do not want to bend down and pick up anything else's waste. Walking home from the jazz lounge well after midnight, I had to dodge the hundreds of unfetched landmines that littered my path, but walking up the red carpet staircase in the late afternoon before my evening shift began, I felt like I was moving into an artistic, delicate, soulful space. I was a co-star in the ambient jazz ensemble of Van Dyke characters, along with the musicians, cocktail waitresses, and other bartenders.

There really was no question as to who my favorite co-workers were at the Van Dyke—the musicians. The cast changed during the weekends when the jazz lounge brought in big names from New York City, Chicago and St. Louis, but on the weeknights there was a set schedule of local musicians who personally colored their respective nights. My favorite evening of music was on Tuesday, when pianist Eddie Higgins played with bassist Don Wilner.

There was hardly anyone in the jazz lounge on Tuesday nights besides a few locals in the know and a couple of stragglers from out of town. It wasn't that the music was bad; on the contrary, I felt it was the best that we offered. But Tuesday was the one night people in South Beach took off to get ready to party the rest of the week. I liked a slow bar on these nights, as it allowed me plenty of time to listen to the music instead of mixing cocktails and pouring glasses of wine all night long like I did on Thursday, Friday, and Saturday evenings.

Upstairs at the Van Dyke on Tuesday nights became my soul's place of worship; it was the one place in South Beach where I felt wholly connected with my environment and myself. My work nights always began with watching the sunset through the second-story windows of the jazz lounge, shadows of dying light creeping upon the facades of light pastel art deco buildings, making them seem like starlets done up for one more role before fading back into obscurity, the soothing heat of red darkness expanding over turquoise sea.

As the overall debauchery of South Beach continued to assault my psyche, the Van Dyke became more and more important to me. I picked up extra shifts so I could spend more time around the music and the musicians. I loved their stories, their melodies, and the way they played together on stage in perfect rhythm, feeding off the energy of the crowd and the cozy elegance of the lounge itself. They were a spiritual river that flowed nightly through the fertile physical place, meandering off into different sounds and textures, branching off into solo instrumental tributaries, and finally bringing it all back down into one jazzy waterfall that poured over the eardrum, saturating the audience with a mastery of beat in time.

Upstairs
— at the —
Van Dyke Café

Live Jazz Nightly

Since 1994

Shows start:
9, 10:30 PM & 12 AM
Sunday-Thursday $3
10, 11:30 PM & 1AM
Fri & Sat: $6

"South Florida's Premier Jazz Club"-Matt Schudel, Fort Lauderdale News/Sun Sentinel
"Best Jazz Club in Miami"- New Times Magazine
Jazz Calendar for February 1999

Sunday	Monday	Tuesday	Wednesday	Thursday	Friday	Saturday
	1 The Legendary Johnny O'Neal *piano & vocal*	2 Eddie Higgins *piano* Don Wilner *bass*	3 Guy Fasciani *piano* Don Wilner *bass*	4 *Hardbop Special* Pete Minger, Dave Hubbard, Jesse Jones, *and the* Don Wilner Trio	5 The Noel Friedline Trio *with* Renee Dickerson	6 The Noel Friedline Trio *with* Renee Dickerson
7 Raul Midon *vocals with the* Don Wilner Quartet *featuring* Billy Ross	8 Eddie Higgins *piano* Don Wilner *bass*	9 Eddie Higgins *piano* Don Wilner *bass*	10 Fred Hersch *piano* Don Wilner *bass* James Martin *drums*	11 Fred Hersch *piano* Don Wilner *bass* James Martin *drums*	12 The Billy Marcus Quartet *and special guest vocalist*	13 The Billy Marcus Quartet *and special guest vocalist*
14 Raul Midon *vocals with the* Don Wilner Quartet *featuring* Billy Ross	15 Mike Gerber *piano* Don Wilner *bass*	16 Guy Fasciani *piano* Jim Kessler *bass*	17 Merideth d'Ambrosio *vocals* Eddie Higgins *piano* Don Wilner *bass*	18 *Hardbop Special* Pete Minger, Dave Hubbard, Jesse Jones, *and the* Don Wilner Trio	19 Roseanna Vitro *vocals* Mike Renzi *piano* Don Wilner *bass*	20 Roseanna Vitro *vocals* Mike Renzi *piano* Don Wilner *bass*
21 Raul Midon *vocals with the* Don Wilner Quartet *featuring* Billy Ross	22 Mark Marineau *piano* Don Wilner *bass*	23 Eddie Higgins *piano* Don Wilner *bass*	24 Guy Fasciani *piano* Don Wilner *bass*	25 *Hardbop Special* Pete Minger, Dave Hubbard, Jesse Jones, *and the* Don Wilner Trio	26 The Raul Midon Group	27 The Raul Midon Group
28 Raul Midon *vocals with the* Don Wilner Quartet *featuring* Billy Ross						

Ask your server about our mailing list.

Rev. 1/14/99

One slow Tuesday night at the end of March, after the patrons and musicians had all left for their hotel rooms or homes, I took some extra time to clean the bar and re-stock. I soaked in the smell of cigar butts, leftover perfume, red wine, and cognac. This night, after Eddie Higgins stirred my soul all evening long with his deft piano playing, I had made the decision to leave South Beach. It was almost two o'clock in the morning as I sat on a stool at the end of the long wood bar sipping a twenty year old tawny port, while the street lamps of Lincoln Road glowed in the South Florida atmosphere.

There was nothing quite like setting up the bar upstairs at the Van Dyke, or closing it down well after midnight: looking out at the throngs of dressed-up bodies walking or posing on Lincoln Road with the taste of overpriced sushi, mojitos, Cuban cigars, and the sea swirling and inter-playing upon their palates. I must admit it was an intoxicating stage, one that could make or break your ego if you allowed it to be totally real. And it was real for a lot of people, a lot of souls lost in the camera flashes, the shark stares, and the gusty winds bending the heads of thousands of palm trees along the pastel strip.

But for me, the root was not people inside the jazz lounge at the Van Dyke, but jazz bringing people into place to blossom for a time together. For that is what *being in place* does, even in a microcosmic sense, it allows one to get closer to that step of brilliance that exists within them, the place where the swinging hinge of eternity, a child's urge to play on the see-saw, the rise and fall of the living road, finally glides into fluid, motionless balance—until the song ends, and like in the game of musical chairs, we begin the journey all over again.

American Rhythm
(A Quick Hit from Miami to Boulder)

Indian Shrimp

It had been seven months since I last traversed the great expanse of America. But first, I had to cross out of Florida, out of the heat and vacation wasteland, into the real South of Alabama and Mississippi. I needed some good old-fashioned Southern Hospitality and old charm to romance me back to life after five months in Miami.

Lucky for me a rich couple from Coconut Grove needed someone to drive their older model BMW out to their daughter who was going to be starting as a freshman at the University of Colorado in Boulder. She had taken a first class plane ride out to her new school. Thus I got a free car and a small stipend for expenses for one week, and all I had to do was drive the car out to the land of the Rockies and make sure it got to their daughter in the same condition as I picked it up in.

As I hit Pensacola, I knew Mobile wasn't far, and once I passed through that murky industrial city, I decided to drive along the coast of Mississippi. I stopped in a small town, Pass Christian, and checked into a Bed and Breakfast: The Inn at The Pass, a grand but cozy Southern home of Victorian beauty.

After a long, cool shower, I walked to a café down by the harbor, and dined on a tasty fried shrimp dinner while a gang of stray beach cats mulled around my table. Gulf shrimp are small, but there were close to a hundred of them on my platter for only five dollars, so even though I was on a budget, I decided to order a beer. I took a swig from the sweating bottle, swirled the hoppy suds around the inside of my mouth, relaxed back against my chair and admired the classic wooden shrimp trawlers floating in the harbor. After another sip, I looked around at the other people in the café. It seemed we'd all been lulled into sweet submission by the Gulf's sultry rhythm.

Stuffed, I walked back to the Inn at The Pass, and after a sway on the porch swing, fell asleep atop my stately bed to the sounds of rain and thunder clapping jazz along the Mississippi Sound. I woke early, walking out onto the freshly lit white sand to wake tide pools with seagulls. On the beach, my path crossed with a rather dignified gentleman, complete with cane, derby hat and glasses. We started talking, and after I told him about the tasty dinner I had last night, he proclaimed, "Those shrimp probably came from India." I found that comment rather odd, but he just smiled and starting talking about meditation, and how every morning he gets up at this time to walk on the beach, because, "It clears my mind of all the gook that's built up over the years."

He said he's lived in Pass Christian the last thirty years, but still feels like a stranger, "Because you see young friend, this town's made up of old Southerners and old Southern money, and no man from Missora will ever be excepted into that long-time fraternity. But no matter, this walk I take along the beach every morning is friend enough." I agreed with him. What did man need with money and fraternities anyway?

I went back to the Inn at The Pass and had a hearty breakfast of cheese grits, maple sausage, pecan-glazed French toast, and overgrown strawberries with cream. It was a grand spread. All of the other guests at the table, mostly senior citizens with mobile homes and one young couple from Atlanta, kept saying, "Oh it must be nice to be so free."

One old woman came up to me as she and her husband were getting ready to leave and gave me a pamphlet on Jesus Christ and some flyers from her church, saying,

"Now read this Jake because I want to see you in heaven."
And I said, "Maybe we're already there." She got annoyed
at that. I guess she didn't believe anything as sublime as
heaven could actually be here with us. I got up and gave
her a big hug, and could tell that made her feel better
because she let out a great big "Oooohh" as I squeezed
her. She blessed me and said, "Jesus will be watchin over
your soul." That kind of freaked me out. Not because I
thought Jesus would be stalking me, but because she
must have thought that I needed help. Hell, I guess we all
need a little help.

Sour Mash Blues

There was no time to be down over it though because I
was on my way to Memphis, where I was going to sample
some of the best blues and ribs in the world. On the drive
to Memphis, up a Mississippi highway, I felt like I was
marching toward an artistic birthplace my soul needed to
pay homage to. I started thinking about all the great souls
who had suffered and wailed through the early years of
America's purest art forms, Blues and Jazz, and who had
in their tireless soul-searching efforts to express
themselves also influenced many of the great writers and
musicians who influenced me. Art is without question a
series of hand-me-downs, and everyone who becomes a
part of the family has a long line of ties they had better
not forget. That includes paying your respects to artistic
homes and Memphis is one of them.

Coming into Memphis I saw that it was a sprawling city,
so I headed straight downtown. It was a little past
America's dinnertime and not quite party time, so the
streets of Memphis were mine. I walked down by the river
and watched a paddleboat churn through the water. I

couldn't help feeling romanced, like I was tapping into something very real, and religiously Southern.

Something I noticed real quickly was the many pickpockets and petty thieves walking around Beale Street. It was obvious to me, because I used to live in Newark, New Jersey, in a neighborhood full of them. But these rich folk, strolling around with their fat wallets sticking out and Gucci bags slung over slender shoulders, I don't think they had a clue.

Once again, I can notice these things but when you're out there on the streets of America there ain't nothing you can do but recognize and move on. Because even if I went up to one of those rich couples walking around like the world was a jackpot they just won, they may or may not believe me. They may even think that I was trying to scam them. Which I would never do because I'm happy enough walking the line between the thieves and the rich, which sometimes is a truly blurry line, if you catch my drift.

The only drift I wanted to catch was the hickory, molasses, slow roasted goodness of ribs and baked beans and some rich, creamy Cole slaw. I went into a little corner barbecue abode that had big wooden tables with sauce stains soaked into the swirling knots, and sat by the window, letting the sounds of B.B. King's Blues Place simmer inside of me, and by the time the ribs came, I was in Memphis, the Memphis of artistic, and romantic, Southern legend.

I ate the ribs with caution (not letting any of the meat go to waste) and reckless abandon (getting sauce all over my lips and chin and some on the table to leave my own mark) and when they and the beans and the slaw were done, I sat back, letting the moment seep into me. The night was mine. It had always been. And lately, after all that stuffed-up sweltering of Miami, I was able to wallow in the openness of my road once again.

After dinner settled, I walked through the streets of Memphis wafting into Blues bar after Blues bar, until I found a little hole-in-the-wall joint off the main drag where it seemed the locals and people who really tripped on Blues hung out. The walls were stained a dark yellow from tobacco smoke, and everyone in the room seemed to be massaging a rocks glass with either bourbon or sour mash whiskey in it.

I sat at a small table in the corner of the room and took a sip of my Old Fashioned. Looking around at the other people in the room, it was then that I realized; in Memphis, ribs are cooked real slowly, and the Blues even slower, until the meat falls right off the bone, and into your soul, heavy and sweet, like the flow of molasses poured from a jar.

I sat there for the rest of the night, swirling in tobacco circles, tripping on the digging riffs and lyrics of an old black man, who, as his spirit rose to the ceiling, the roof, like an old friend, brought him back down. In a world of Blues, you cannot escape what makes you real.

The Anderson House

After a decent night's sleep at a cheap hotel outside of Memphis, I ate breakfast at a Waffle House (pecan waffle, grits, orange juice and coffee) and then pulled back onto the interstate still slightly dazed from all the Blues and smoke of the previous night. I drove toward the Ozarks, in the "Natural State" of Arkansas.

When I pulled into Heber Springs, it was a little like being in the Wild West – narrow, dusty streets, old two and three story buildings lining the sides of downtown. I had made reservations at The Anderson House, a sprawling country inn with about twenty rooms. Bed and breakfasts and country inns can be very inexpensive during off-season. They are still a bit more expensive than youth hostels and cheap interstate motels, but offer much more comfort and ambience and usually a hearty breakfast.

The proprietor of The Anderson House was a very tall fellow, about 6'7" if I remember correctly. It turns out, he had recently bought the place after living in Colombia for a few years, where he met and married a Colombian woman. The two of them lived at The Anderson House with their little girl, who was very cute and always talking to me in Spanish and laughing, because she knew I was just a dumb American and only knew American English. She was only three, but had already learned English, Spanish, and "is now starting to take French lessons," her father proclaimed proudly.

I ate at a local restaurant the proprietor recommended. I had sautéed Lake Trout over long grain wild rice, and a nice conversation with a young couple that were going to get married after they graduated from high school. This amazed me, because at twenty-four years old, I didn't feel ready for a committed relationship.

The young couple kept saying, "Why in the world did you come to Heber Springs?" When I replied that I had lived in South Beach, Miami, they responded, "I don't see why in the world you ever left." Though they had only seen South Beach on MTV. Besides, I always leave places for the same reason, things get tiring and I don't want to fall asleep.

After a restful evening reading Walt Whitman's *Leaves of Grass* in a big comfy chair by the fireplace with a mug of black cherry tea, I walked up the long, creaky, winding, wooden staircase and hit the sack. I awoke to a blissfully sunny morning. One of those cockcrows where the air is crisp and cool and you feel spring creep into your cells to tell you that death is only a temporary state that leads to an ever-blooming eternity.

My tall host cooked up a great Southern breakfast: blueberry pancakes with real maple syrup, bacon, hash browns, and topped it all off with a warm peach cobbler. After brushing my teeth and packing up, I played a game of hide-and-go-seek with their daughter and golden lab in the backyard bramble. Then, I once again said good-bye to new found friends and pulled onto the up-and-down roads of Northern Arkansas and on into Missouri where I stayed at a Red Roof Inn off of the interstate for $19.99 and then up onto the county roads of Kansas with their beautiful wide-open stretches of corn fields and winding streams.

Deondra's Ghost

The only thing I knew of Kansas was a beautiful girl named Deondra, whom I had met when I was sixteen and went to play in the AAU Basketball National Championship in San Antonio. I played for a team called the Jersey Jayhawks, which was made up of a bunch of street wise, wise-ass white kids who could shoot three pointers like they were going out of style and a great agile power forward from Puerto Rico. It turned out that at the same time all of us sixteen year old boys from all over the country were in San Antonio for the basketball tournament, there was also an FHA convention going on, who if you don't know, are the Future Homemakers of America.

At night, after the games, our coaches would drop us off at The Riverwalk, an elaborate indoor/outdoor mall with cobblestone walkways, outdoor cafes, and gondolas stroking in and out of the canal along the storefronts. I met Deondra one night as my friend Greg and I were eating at one of the cafes. She walked by our table with a friend and I quickly read her name tag and said, "Deondra, that's a really dope name." The word dope was big with us North Jersey punks back then, and a beautiful girl like Deondra, long flowing hair the color of a ripe cornhusk and cute little sun freckles blossoming on her face, should have just looked at me and said, "My, my." But she

walked over to the table, sat down, and we spent the rest of the night talking on a bench by the canal. At one point, she rubbed my head, because I had a flat top back then, and said, "It feels like porcupine quills."

That was the first time in my young life that I ever got high without smoking or drinking anything. The first time I realized girls could open up a whole new world: a world that knew no time or space, only the moment. But there was no sign of Deondra among the rows of dead corn. I wouldn't have guessed there was any civilization outside of Wichita, if I hadn't seen a sign that read, "Historic Lindsborg 7 Miles."

Lindsborg is a small art colony, which was originally settled by the Swedish. It has a charming downtown, with little shops along cobblestone streets, and by the looks of it, the people still work hard at preserving their Swedish heritage. In fact, I was staying at the Swedish Country Inn, decorated like something out of a Hans Christian Andersen novel and kind of "It's a Small World after All."

I borrowed a bike from the inn and pedaled around the town. I found a timeworn windmill by a lazy stream, where I decided to skip some rocks upon the surface of the water. I got a five skipper one time, and took that as a good sign. I don't know why exactly. It's not like the number five holds any kind of special significance for me. My favorite numbers are seven and twenty-one, but I remember as a kid that if you could get your rock to skip more than three times, you were doing something right.

Later, I ate dinner at a Swedish bistro, The Vas Club, which was a restaurant in front where I ate a steak marinated with some kind of Swedish sauce, and then after dinner, went to the lounge tucked away in the back of the building. The bartender, who used to play quarterback for the local college football team, told me the lounge got packed on the weekends with old Swedish couples whooping it up to a piano player who played traditional folk songs.

There was no live music on this night, but the bartender had tuned the dial to the local Jazz station. I nestled up to the bar, sipped my glass of red wine, and took it all in. I was glad this place existed, and glad there was a fireplace, because it was early March and still pretty darn cold in Kansas.

Boulders

After a long stretch of rolling country roads through the western part of Kansas, I spilled onto a wide-open highway heading towards Denver. I felt like a free fugitive of life. Up ahead, a coyote ran across the highway.

Passing the industrial part of Denver wasn't all that inspiring, but then I found the local jazz station and that rhythmic part of me started to come alive. I accelerated over a steep pass and saw the Rockies straight ahead.

I cruised into Boulder as the last peaks of light evaporated behind the Flatirons. I checked into the Boulder International Hostel and went up to my room to shower. After relaxing under the nozzle for a while, I looked out the steamed-up bathroom window and saw it had started to snow. I walked back to my room, opened the blinds, and peered straight up past the streetlights to that divine light coming down off the white covered mountains of the Colorado rooftop.

I went out and walked around the small area of shops and restaurants by the University of Colorado, ducking into a pub to grab a hot turkey sandwich and a Porter. The waitress brought the pint of dark treacly beer, and I licked the foam and took a sip—fireplaces, pine meadows, icy streams, coffee, chocolate and licorice—my senses were heightened, proving that I am a travel junky.

The next morning I awoke to a sunny seventy-degree day. The snow on the grass had almost all melted, but it was still packed up in the mountains. The college kids were out walking around with shorts and sweaters on or loading snowboards onto SUV's. I was content to wander around up in the Flatirons for the next few days.

Sitting on boulders at the top of the trails and looking out became my fascination. I saw small towns nestled between great encampments of rock and clear blue lakes surrounded by tall Evergreens. One day, I hiked up Baird's Bell and sat down on a moss-covered rock. I looked out into the long drawn-out valley of grass and bushes interspersed with powder. It was almost foggy from the heaviness of oncoming snow in the air, when I wrote:

Vapor vision
High in mountains

Bird song
Curves through valley
Human hooves
Sully muddy trail

Height lessons
The fall below

I was getting high walking around up in all that thin air. One day, I sprinted down a hill and damn near killed myself when I slipped on a piece of ice and tumbled down the valley, but I just remember the tumbling and not the hitting of the frozen ground, just the whirling over and over again as my eyes peaked out from beneath my wool hat into an upside-down, right-side up world of white and pale drifting blue.

I spent many a day plopping around the Boulder Creek trying to cross the rushing water. The stones and rocks made shiny bridges. I traversed them constantly. Each path presenting a new and interesting challenge to the child I had now become. It's funny, when we first fall in love we are very much like children, but as time goes on, we begin to face love with mature manners, like grown-ups would. Then the love withers, so we become even more serious and try to make it work, and then, it drowns completely. Sometimes, I think only children can truly love one another. To them, the world is an amusement park, not something to be won or lost.

I wrote a poem to Shakespeare one day:

> Today,
> From a small bridge in Boulder,
> I look down onto the nothingness
> Of water
>
> Strands of molecules
> Floating together
> In liquefied form
>
> Parts
> Of a whole
> Going from place to place,
> Flowing in
> And through time
>
> An endless play
> of fluidity.

And as I sat looking out from the top of a mountain, I wrote this to Gary Snyder:

> If there is nothing,
> And the mountains
> And rivers
> Are nothingness visions
> Of awakened emptiness

Then,
Where does the snow
At the tip of the world go
When it melts away?

Kerouac's Sax

At a coffeehouse in downtown Boulder, there was going to be a reading in honor of Jack Kerouac's 77th birthday. To personally honor this momentous occasion, I visited a local bar and had a couple of glasses of Port wine before walking through the invigorating valley night air to the place where I and others would be holding testament to one of the great voices of our time.

I walked inside the place, which had a nice Rocky Mountain vibe, wide open and full of wood, smelling of cinnamon, nutmeg, and coffee grinds. I ordered a hot apple cider. I was hoping there would be a bunch of crazy poets passing around jugs of wine, but the place remained abstract and heady. I read a passage from *The Dharma Bums* after female beat poet and professor, Anne Waldman, read a passage from *On The Road*. I was disappointed with the lack of energy. It wasn't very "Beat like."

I walked back to the hostel through what now seemed like a deep solaceful night. I stopped and sat next to a scruffy old man in ragged clothes who was blowing sax on the street, and thought, "This is how you pay tribute to Kerouac." I dropped a dollar in the guy's hat and pulled out a pen:

The beat
Sweet and neat

Floatin' by fools on concrete

Moon in sky
Stars love Jazz
That spiritual razz-ma-tazz
Of stray cats
Wandering home
To that throne
Of meaningless brilliance

Sitting on the ground
With fountains turned off in winter
I'm thirsty
And formlessly cold
With my coat half-zipped

There it is Jack. I hoped you liked it. Happy Birthday.

Get Outta Town Clowns
(Butte, Montana)

"It's too bad things didn't work out in Portland," Steve said.

"Yeah, I guess I had always envisioned it being different out there," I replied. "I was surprised by how industrial it was."

"I loved the strong dark coffee though."

"I know you did," I replied as we cut through the vast mountainous landscape at 70 m.p.h. "We had some good times out there though. We met that Italian guy, Alessandro, at the youth hostel and all of those wild homeless people in the park that we slept in those last few days before we decided to go back East."

"That apartment was too small for the both of us," Steve noted somberly.

"It was a small studio," I replied. "Not a large studio like the ad said. It's too bad we lost our deposit or maybe we could have stuck around a bit longer until we found jobs."

"This country makes me feel small," Steve let out in a voice that seemed too unsure for him. "I think I'd rather be back in that apartment or in that café on the corner drinking strong coffee."

"Believe me," I responded. "The first time I drove across America, I got pretty anxious about being immersed in all this emptiness."

"I don't mean America. I mean Montana."

"It is a lot different than Jersey out here," I answered.

"Yeah it is."

I looked over at Steve because there had been a sense of isolation and uneasiness in the way he had spoken those last few phrases. He was a gritty surf punk who grew up thrashing waves on his short board along the Jersey shore. I had met him in college down in Florida, where we took to each other like long lost brothers the moment we were introduced. Steve smoked a ton of cigarettes, and at times could seem jittery to the untrained eye, but as a poet and fellow Jersey boy, I saw through that superficial movement to the steely depth in his concentrated green eyes. Thus the sound of listlessness in his voice struck me as we headed East through the big sky territory.

We drove in silence for the next half hour or so, until the gas tank of my 1979 Ford Fairmount station-wagon read near empty, and I pulled off of the interstate to find a filling station in a place named Butte. There happened to be a service station with a little convenience store attached to it less than a quarter mile from the exit. As I filled the tank with gas, Steve went inside to use the restroom and purchase a cup of coffee. When he came back outside, there were two girls who seemed to be around 18 or 19 years old in tow behind him.

For some reason, I thought these girls were going to be trouble. Steve and I were both in our early twenties. He had short bleached blond hair that was almost white and sported a nose ring, while I had a head full of long blond hair that extended to my mid back. You could say that we looked a bit out of place standing there next to an old, beat-up station wagon packed to the gills with camping equipment, dirty clothes, and art supplies parked at a gas station in Montana.

"Did you fill her up?" Steve asked.

"Yeah," I replied. "I see you've picked up a couple of sand sharks in your wake."

Steve turned around as the girls were almost to the car and then looked at me and said, "They started talking to me when I asked for the coffee. They're interested in our trip. What we're doing all the way out here."

"So what are you guys doing out here?" The shorter of the two girls asked after overhearing our conversation.

"We're on a nomadic expedition," I answered.

"You got fishin gear in there?" The taller girl asked while looking over at our vehicle.

"There's no fishing gear in there but a lot of art supplies," Steve responded.

"We don't have a lotta artists round here, but a lotta people in Montana like to fish," the shorter girl said.

"I'm sure the fishing out here must be really good," I stated. "But we're just passing through on our way back across the country."

"That's a shame because we could use a couple a guys like you round here to liven things up," the taller girl said with a sexy smile.

"Yeah, you should stay a while," the shorter girl added with a mischievous giggle.

It was right around this time that I noticed a guy who was about the same age as the girls poke his head out of the gas station store. His eyes met mine from across the parking lot. The only thing in his eyes was hostility for the two strangers talking to the local girls. I tried to get Steve's attention, but after only having me to talk with for two days straight on the road the girls had waylaid his attention. Maybe it was because I had traveled a lot more than Steve, but my nomad senses were tingling, telling me to get the hell out of there.

After listening to Steve and the local girls have a half-assed conversation for about ten minutes, which was really Steve lecturing earnestly about art and the girls spouting ridiculous sexual innuendo that could not possibly ever come to fruition, I noticed what seemed like a parade of jacked-up pickup trucks pulling into the parking lot. It was like watching a pack of steelhead trout with bad intentions streaming into a shallow pool in order to feast on a couple of minstrel male water skippers who for some strange reason were trying to mate with some homegrown female crawdads. The next thing I knew our station wagon was surrounded. The two girls looked at the trucks and then at each other and almost simultaneously blurted out, "Oh shit," before they walked quickly away from us and back into the convenience store.

Then Steve turned to look at me, and I saw in his eyes that he now realized the rapid gravity of the situation. Yet I also saw that he wasn't scared, and neither was I, because we were from New Jersey where we had both been in our fair share of fights, and now lived in Florida, where we had both surfed with our fair share of sharks. What I think confounded us the most was how quickly this mob of monster trucks and their teamsters had assembled before us. At least with a shark you got some warning, as a fellow surfer would invariably yell out, "There's a guy in a grey flannel suit out here!"

For a while we just stood there peering out at the glaring assembly, waiting for someone from their party to make a move. We were close enough to the gas pumps that I figured they wouldn't try to run us over. However it was Montana and several of the trucks had gun racks with rifles stationed upon them. Eventually, the door of the largest monster truck opened and a short scrawny guy about our age jumped down from his mammoth machine perch. I looked over at Steve and we both had to try to keep from laughing, as the Napoleon-like figure barely kept his feet after making the leap.

The guy wore baggy black jeans and a wife beater that had the word "insane" printed on it. He sported a buzz cut that made him look like a white supremacist. We would later learn that Butte was in fact the home to many white supremacists.

He strode toward us with a pompous lethargic manner. His gait was no accident but was made to deliver a message to us, and that message was "This is my territory." Finally, he completed his saunter over to us. When I say over to us, I mean that he stood with his nose pressed into my Adam's apple. Again, this was a deliberate move to show us that he had absolutely no fear because this was his place. He had chosen me because I was six foot three and well built at the time. Steve was about five foot nine and wiry.

What happened next will always live on in my memory for its shear veracity and simplicity. The guy cocked his head upward, stared straight into my eyes, and addressed the both of us when he calmly stated, "Get outta town clowns." I remember feeling as if everything else in the world, the cars and tractor trailers careening by on the interstate, the other local shaved-head males and their girlfriends who had stepped out of their trucks and assembled around us, the crows sitting on the telephone wires had all frozen as Montana's modern version of Napoleon uttered that perfect locational message to us.

The guy then repositioned his head so that his nose once again poked into my Adam's apple for the next minute or so. The only sound I heard during this time was a crow's wings flapping overhead as it left its perch along the wires and flew off into the Western horizon, which was now a tad darker blue than when we had arrived and infused with light orange and red pre-orgasmic strokes of color as the sun began to finalize its descent into the deep vast salt water that ebbed and flowed beyond the mountains and desert far to the left. At this point I managed to glance over at Steve who was inwardly fuming, and who I guessed was about ten seconds away from unhinging the gasoline hose from its compartment, spraying the guy with said liquid and then throwing his lit cigarette onto him. This however would not have been a good decision, so I gathered up all of the yin energy I had stored up from our time visiting the West Coast and said to our new diminutive acquaintance and anyone else who would listen, "Well then, we'll be on our way."

I moved away from the guy and shoved Steve towards the passenger side front door. Then I walked around the anterior of the car over to the driver's side, opened the door, looked around one last time to appreciate that all of the eyes of the local posse were still burned into me, got inside, inserted the key into the ignition and turned it. As we drove out of the gas station parking lot, a caravan of monster trucks began to appear behind our station wagon. This caravan followed us back out onto the interstate and stayed with us until the next exit, which was positioned at the Butte city limits. There the trucks all turned off the interstate like one long curling fly-fishing line heading towards an eddy, as Steve and I sped into the hazy Eastern horizon---two thousand miles away from the familiarity and security of the polluted waves we grew up on.

Jake and Steve "The Clowns"

Not another Literary Reference to Key West
(Key West, Florida)

The last time I did a stint down in Key West my friend Stro and I stopped at a liquor store and bought a bottle of dark rum, some orange juice, and a lime from a small market, drove over to the "other" part of town, parked on a dim side street where some of the local denizens were hanging out, took the various ingredients from the shopping bag and mixed a kind of poor man's *Planter's Punch* that we each took turns swigging from the orange juice container.

An old black woman wearing a purple nightgown and a fake pearl necklace rode over to us on a child's size pink Huffy bicycle and asked us, "If I go to my house and get a container will you pour me some of that concoction you got into it?" I said "Sure," and she pedaled away. About ten minutes later she was back with what looked like a jelly jar that she had just rinsed out but still had some jam clinging to the sides: from the dark ruby color and light seeds I surmised it must have been raspberry. I poured some of our improvised mixture into her jar. She thanked me graciously and asked, "What's your name?"

"Jake," I answered. "And this is my friend Stro."

"Nice to meet you fellas. I'm Esther," the woman replied shaking both of our hands at the same time, while she skillfully held onto the jelly jar with the few teeth that she had left. Once she relinquished our hands she took the jar in her right hand and tilted it to her lips, taking a deep relaxed pull from its smooth wide mouth.

As she talked to us I understood that she was drunk. Not bad drunk, but local chatty drunk. We spent a good amount of time with Esther as she told us some of the history of her neighborhood and how she was going to a party later tonight at her favorite club. "Well, it's not really a club, more like a house that's been turned into a speakeasy, a place for the local drunks who can't afford to drink in the tourist bars on Duval St. or any of the other trendy waterin holes poking up in good ole' Key West." She told us how the Jamaicans and Haitians were being run out of the city to make room for more "Yuppy-type housin."

Then she went on, "We ain't used to seeing a couple of white boys standing on the corner drinking in our neighborhood. If the cops pass they're going to hassle you, think you're trying to buy drugs from one of us."

Looking around the street it was obvious that there were drug deals going on every ten minutes or so down the block, as cars would pull up, and then the person in the car would hand the person in the street who had just handed them the plastic bag some paper money, and alas drive away to get high somewhere else besides this dingy yet very orderly and quiet neighborhood.

While Stro and I watched the night's events unfold around us, everyone that walked by our unusual trio smiled and said hello to Esther. All of the neighborhood locals were of a darker skin tone than us, and many of them spoke with sharp, broken rhythmic island accents, yet we felt absolutely no hostility or anger directed towards us.

However, a couple of minutes later a group of clean-cut white college age guys wearing their fraternity letters on baseball caps and sporting khaki shorts and polo shirts, went carousing loudly through the neighborhood, bottles of imported beer in their hands, yelling and cursing at each other and anybody else within earshot, and then breaking their empties on the ground.

Esther looked at them and then back at us saying, "There, those people are gonna be the ones buyin up our neighborhoods in the future and moving us out because we're the ones who they say drive the real estate down.

Well, I may be an old drunk but at least I gots enough common sense to keep my misgivings to myself. I ain't messin with nobody's sleep."

We drank with Esther for a while longer and then she gave us each a soulful hug goodbye and told us to stop by her neighborhood anytime we wanted. "You boys are always welcome on these here streets," she said. "I'll spread the word and let everyone know. That's how it is here. Everyone's seen ya'll here with me tonight, so if they see ya'll again they'll give you the nod. That nod means it's all gooood."

Later that night while Stro and I were walking down Duval Street, among a seething sea of drunk and stoned white bodies with patches of scintillating red sunburn decorating their swerving frames like rust on an old junker, we didn't get one hello from anybody. There were thousands of people out partying but not one random hello or even a return of a friendly nod.

Eventually we ran into an older couple who were for some strange reason inquiring of a group of rather loud drunk men, if there was any place to go in Key West that had more of a local's vibe to it. To this question, the trusty leader of this group of intoxicated middle-aged men responded, "Duval Street is where it's at. There's beer and liquor and tits everywhere. Why would you want to go anywhere else?"

After another fifteen minutes of wandering Stro and I bumped into two cops. Stro asked them where the Cuban section of town was or if there was an older more relaxed part of Key West that we could explore. The younger of the two white cops was eager to give us his response, "There isn't a Cuban section, just a couple of restaurants. As for an older part of town, you boys should do your best to stay around Duval Street. Other parts of Key West have got a bad element hanging around. It's not safe for a couple of guys like yourselves if you know what I mean." As he said that a sunburned overweight middle-aged white woman lifted up her shirt and flashed her tits to the cheers of a bunch of intoxicated white college guys. The two cops didn't seem to care.

We walked away from the cops, the tourists and Duval Street in disgust. Without asking one another where we should go, we intuitively walked straight back to where we had met Esther earlier. She wasn't there, so we took the ingredients out of my backpack and mixed up some more of our poor man's *Planter's Punch* and stood contently on the corner sipping our drinks and letting the cool midnight Florida Key breeze filter through our psyches.

We must have stood there drinking for well over an hour, saying hello to the various locals after they gave us the aforementioned nod, before Esther eventually found us. She was drunker than when we had met her before, and so were we. She asked me to "pour some more of that smooth concoction" into her jar, which I deftly obliged.

As the three of us stood there together under the crystal clear light of the three quarter full moon, Esther introduced us to everyone from her neighborhood that walked by: drug dealers, crack heads, members of her congregation, slick young ballers, prostitutes, shopkeepers, her niece Mary, it didn't matter who, she knew them all. Esther was proud of her place in the community. Sure she might have been a drinker, but she was honest. Those bottle-breaking frat boys and cops out on Duval Street, they were the real drunks, drunk on power, a sense of entitlement, and self-absorbed whiteness.

Esther was like the mayor, the communicator of a part of town that the tourists didn't know existed and the city council and real estate planners wanted to tear down to make room for expensive condos and fashionable bars and eateries. She was a link to the past, to a time when people lived in Key West for the characters, and the overall intoxication of the place itself: a simpler time when Disney World was still just in Orlando.

But it's like that in America. We want to get rid of any sense of place that doesn't lure the tourists or make the trendy liberal "bohemian" upper middle class want to move there. It's easy to knock down a section of town that the so-called well-heeled people and ruling bodies declare an eyesore. Then, after it's gone, educated fanciful white writers, who had never actually spent time with the people in their place back in the day, can make up great literary stories about what that location used to be like.

But I've been to Key West, many times. Breathed it in with my own lungs and seen it with my own two eyes. I sipped dark rum and shook even darker hands along the shady back streets. I found those hands worn and welcoming---if a little shaky at times. I appreciated the deep lines ingrained into those hands, as they were navigational drawings that led back to various locales in the Caribbean.

Maybe at this point of their existence one could say they were a little down on their luck, but luck is a thing that is very hard to define or understand merely by exterior appearances. Luck runs deeper than that. Like the distilled sugarcane intoxicates our bloodstream unbeknownst to the voracious world passing by us.

alcohol stained walls of
smoky manic-kinetic energy

early morning drinks
rough sea eyes
drunking wake-up
at sunrise bar

spirits passing issued
on fast-talking
Duval sun-soaked street

deep dream shelter
all thought thugs
wake-up scene sun

all salty
locals begging
for home grown
eccentricity

warm nights blocks
sunday indigenous
solve through streets.

funk and rock
acid pure acid
salty and politics
and streets/greed

one bridge on and off
the island of our reality

The end of America. Sunshine thick foliage thoroughbred white local mentality and air hangs like part-time in energy breezes passing through tourists, locals, debauchery, vice old blue-blood vitalis in old tin with xxx spirit of white college Sunday dress colorful traditions and spirits and scared to dare pastiche south citizens renews

dolphins snort sidly gate hawks scaring in the depths of the back Republic clean blue sky sunny cold clone to covid with soul bottom

Key West Poem on Soda Box

Sweet Tamales at Christmas
(Ft. Worth, Texas to Fort Collins, Colorado)

The night was damp and I had been traveling for three days when I stepped onto the Greyhound bus in Ft. Worth, Texas. I walked toward the back and saw only one seat left. I sat down and the young Chicano guy in the window seat next to me lifted his pierced face from beneath a black hoodie and asked, "What's up?"

"Nothin much," I replied.

"I can't believe I was in this stinkin town for three weeks," he stated. "I can't wait to get back to California, back to my old lady."

I found it odd that this young guy referred to his girlfriend or current wife as his "old lady," but I knew what he meant about Ft. Worth. I had only been in the city for a few hours, but it seemed like its downtown, a place where shiny skyscrapers shot forth from the flat landscape, had been designed by a group of intoxicated Texas oil tycoons who were hell bent on advertising to the eyes of every itinerant soul who had somehow managed to wander into this steely place, just how unwelcome they were here.

"What were you doing in Ft. Worth?" I asked him.

"I came back to settle this thing with my last old lady," he answered. "That bitch took everything but my land. But that's okay. She can have all that other stuff as long as I got my land."

"You got land?"

"Yeah, my papa left me twenty acres west of San Bernardino and that land is gonna be worth a shitload of money one day," he stated proudly.

"Maybe it already is," I added.

"Yeah but I wanna keep it and give it to my kid when he gets older. I got a little boy back in Cali."

"How old is he?" I asked.

"Just turned three," and then like I had suddenly vanished from the material world, he turned to look outside at the late-night ghosts hovering on the Texas plains. Just then some young kid in the back of the bus started yelling in an urban Southern drawl about how there was snow on the ground. But it was not snow, only plains dust highlighted by the moon---for the teardrops of frozen angels do not gather on the pampas but only come to rest on lofty settlements of rock.

I leaned back in my chair and let my head roll and cradle in between the small gap in the seats. Then out of nowhere the young Chicano turned back to me and said, "I can't believe that ho fucked my best friend. I mean shit, you leave your old lady alone with your boy for a couple of hours and when you come back he's bangin her."

"That sucks bro," I said.

"But fuck it. I wasn't gonna kick his ass or nothin. It wasn't his fault. That bitch is hot. Shit, if he left me alone with her and she was his girlfriend, I wouldda fucked her too," he stated bluntly, and then turned his face to the window as if some magnetic pull had drawn his tormented consciousness back to the friendless landscape of wasteland and oil rigs.   I stared into the shadowy patches of scrub-brush.

I woke up as the bus pulled into the Amarillo station. I did not have a watch on, but it felt to me like the space of time that exists between two and four in the morning, when if one is awake and out in the world somewhere, divine consciousness superimposes upon the organic environment blessing the whole world with hazy poetics.

Eventually I decided to get off the bus and walked into the rest area. There were lots of college kids with big suitcases wearing baseball caps pulled down over their bloodshot eyes who all seemed to be getting ready to board buses that would carry them home for the holidays, and middle-aged Mexican men wearing thick flannel shirts and denim jeans sitting around the lobby watching little TV's for a quarter. I walked over to the café, grabbed a table by the window and ordered a stack of pancakes.

As I waited for my breakfast, I watched various travelers shuffle by my table and tried to imagine where they might each be journeying to and for what reason and during that moment I forgot where I was going. This happens from time to time when one lives nomadically. The journeys between places can lead your mind out into the uncharted spaces of your own interior map.

I find this to be a good thing for a writer though, especially the kind of writer that I aim to be, for it is in visiting these unsettled areas within ourselves that we remain able to truly feel and connect with the places of the physical world. Once explored, these inner landscapes become sanctuaries that we can retreat into when our pages desire more creative tributaries leading out to the ocean of thought.

Then I remembered: Winter Park, Colorado. That's where I was headed. I had landed a seasonal job as a bartender at a ski lodge. I had never been to Winter Park before so I had no idea what to expect. During one phone interview the owners had explained to me that one of the biggest perks of the job was a free ski pass and lift tickets to the local mountain, but I didn't ski. I guess that fact hadn't dissuaded me too much because here I was sitting down to an early breakfast in an Amarillo café on my way to the snowy mountains of Colorado.

The pancakes were made from Bisquick and the syrup was artificially flavored goo, but it was warm food in a place that provided endless transient characters for me to study so all in all I enjoyed my meal. I paid my check and made sure to be up at the front of the line when the bus re-opened because the bus driver had made it a point to say that seats were not to be saved.

When the driver gave us the okay to re-board, I walked on and headed towards the middle of the bus where I took a window seat, put my feet up on the aisle seat next to me, and stashed my rucksack and coat under my legs. My last trick to assure some room and privacy during this next phase of the trip was to close my eyes and seep a little drool out of the side of my mouth so that nobody would think of asking me to move over if the bus didn't fill up.

Sure enough I got both seats to myself and slept soundly until the bus came to a stop in the parking lot of "Pablo's Burrito Shack," which was simply an old silver Airstream trailer that had been customized with a kitchen and planted in a dusty gravel parking lot in a sleepy little town on the outskirts of sublime New Mexico mountains. It was dusk and the aura encircling the snow-dusted peaks exuded a rosy glow that warmed my heart. And even though I really had no appetite to speak of, an old Aztec-looking woman with a colorful blanket wrapped around her shoulders sold me three delicious sweet Tamales for a dollar.

After eating my tamales while sitting cross-legged on the ground looking out at the mountains, I got back on the bus and cuddled up real cozy against the window using my coat as a pillow. This coat, a beautiful sharpshooters coat with a quilted lining and thermal sleeves, which I purchased for twenty dollars at an army/navy store in downtown Philadelphia several years ago, has been a trusted and comfortable confidant on many a bus and train trip over the years.

The bus kept stopping in dust-bowl towns where one or two stragglers would jump on, until we finally pulled into what seemed like a larger town and I heard a bunch of people boarding. I stretched out across the two seats with my head down and perpetuated the drool trick once again, but to my surprise tap-tap on my head. I pretended not to feel anything until a big hand shook my shoulder, and when I looked up I saw a large Indian smiling at me.

"Sorry buddy, but this is the only seat left," he said.

"Don't worry about it," I replied.

He was a big guy, and so am I, so we spent the first fifteen minutes maneuvering our legs in such a way that we could both feel comfortable without being romantic. When we finally settled into a cozy position, I reached into my pocket and pulled out a bag of peanut M&M's. "You want one?" I asked him.

"Sure."

I handed him a handful of the sugar coated peanuts and asked, "What's your name?"

"Bob," he answered. "And yours?"

"Jake."

"You know Jake," he began, "I shouldn't even be sitting next to you right now. I was on my way up to Pine Ridge to pick up my son, when this car I bought back in Arizona blew up on me as I started coming down from that pass back there."

"Someone sold you a lemon," I replied.

"You could say that," he said, "but when I get back to Arizona, I'll be having a word with the fella who sold me that lemon, if you know what I mean."

"I think I do," I agreed.

"So where are you from Jake?"

"I grew up in New Jersey, but I've been living kind of nomadically for the last five or six years," I replied. "Most recently, I was living down in Florida."

"And what are you doing on a Greyhound bus rolling through the land of enchantment the week before Christmas?" Bob asked.

"To tell you the truth, right now I have no idea. I guess I'm supposed to be going to Winter Park, Colorado, to work at a ski lodge," I answered. "But now that I'm sitting next to you and speaking it out loud to someone other than myself, I get the feeling that this trip is going to have a different ending."

"Sounds like you're either trying to forget something or in the process of finding a new path," Bob said in a very serious tone.

"All I know is that there is something about traveling that accelerates my learning process," I replied, "so when I get the longing to go, I just go. I could say that it doesn't really matter where, but the fact is, once I get going I realize that it's totally about where I am. Thus I always give my intuition plenty of room to lead me roaming."

Bob nodded at me like a soul who understood that one's intuition was the only thing to be trusted in this world. "You know Jake, my wife and my son, along with the rest of my people all live up on the Pine Ridge Reservation. Yet that place has never been my home, and it never will be. As much as I have tried over the years to make a life for myself at that place with them, I just can't do it. That's cause I know in my heart that my people's true land, our ancestral home was taken from us a long time ago."

I may not have been an American Indian, but I could understand how someone could feel displaced and then hit the road in order to find, even if only for small patches of time, places that conveyed some deeper sense of place to them. I am not talking about another hometown, because we all only get one of those per lifetime, but somewhere where our souls feel that they belong at any given moment.

"As an Indian, I now have two choices," Bob began. "The first is to allow my soul to be banished on that reservation. The second, is to continue to follow my own road. This road is a lonely one, yet this isolation that I feel, this total displacement of myself from my native land and people, has dug deep lines of irrigation within me, allowing the healing waters of my ancestors' spiritual wisdom to flow within my heart. As I travel around this country, I see nothing but displaced souls using constructed spaces as the means to an end that will never come without a true identification and connection with the natural place they live. This is my people's predicament up on Pine Ridge as well."

My current thoughts coincided exactly with what Bob was expounding upon, as during his diatribe I could not help but remember the few trips back to New Jersey that I had taken over the years and the disconnection I had felt with my family and friends who had never left the small familiar area we grew up in, after I had traveled through and lived in so many other places. It was not that I felt disconnected from who I was or the specific place where I had been raised; on the contrary, I felt that I had a better understanding of who I was and the distinct environment where I had grown up because of my broader experiences of other locales and their different nuances.

Yet I felt that my family and friends, although exhibiting all of the superficial local socio-cultural conditionings and trappings, really lacked any deep sense of how where they were born and raised was unique compared to the rest of the world. This ignorance of exact place in relation to other different places lent them all a very vacant nostalgic albeit sometimes argumentative feel of pride towards North Jersey, but lacked any intimate poetic embrace that they could share and celebrate with me during my visits.

"To be honest Jake," Bob continued, "and I feel that you know this, there are no separate physical and spiritual places, only whole places where living souls create out from. Many mistakes have been made by people against the environment, against this land that drew us all to it with its vast energy and universal creation story. But unless we learn from those mistakes and begin to start building a better future for this land and its people, all of the hardships, sufferings, and the injustices will have no meaning. An important part of this learning process will be for people to realize that every place has a story to relate to the people that live there. When those people deeply inherit that story and are then able to pass its essence on to others that is when the place becomes a home to them."

Bob was right. It was people's ability to open up to and poetically express the essence of a place that lent those people within that place a distinct feeling of mythology and culture. But without a deep connection to place and natural land there can be no mythology and no culture: there can be no living creation story to take part in together. Thus we get what the industrialization and modernization of American land and the displacement of its native peoples have brought to bear: spiritual, cultural and environmental infertility.

Bob went on, "My people have a belief that the sacred hoop has been broken and it can only be mended when enough of the ancestors are reborn into this world. When these souls realize who they are and why they are here, they will unite and work to bring peace and prosperity back into our sacred places."

"I think that I might have met some of those great souls along my way," I replied.

"I hope so," Bob said sullenly, as he stopped talking and stared out into the vast landscape of rock, sand, sky and all the magical places in between.

We sat in silence for a while but eventually resumed our conversation as our bus rolled through northern New Mexico and southern Colorado and then on up into Denver. It turned out that the bus Bob was supposed to transfer to in Denver was the same as mine. However, my final stop would be Fort Collins whereas Bob would stay on that bus and head up through northern Colorado into Cheyenne, Wyoming, where his ex-wife would pick him up and drive him another seven hours through the mountains up into the Pine Ridge Reservation. There, he'd finally be able to spend time with his son; after all, it was now only a few days until Christmas.

There were only five people on the new bus we boarded together in Denver, which had a very funny black bus driver who laid out the rules of the coach (what drivers call the Greyhound bus) to us, in a just don't do this or this sort of way and we'll all get along fine kind of thing. During our ride, Bob started talking to an old hobo who was heading to Cheyenne, and it turned out that in some crazy way they were third cousins. Bob told his new found cousin that I was on a vision quest, and that our time together was helping to bring that vision into clarity.

I stepped off the bus at the Fort Collins Greyhound station at around 9:30 p.m. just as it began to snow. Bob stepped from the bus and helped me pull my rucksack from the underneath compartment and then gave me a great bear hug and said that he'd see me again somewhere down the road. The bus pulled away and I walked towards the station in utter darkness with my rucksack on my back. As I drew close to the building I realized that the station was closed.

I could see downtown Fort Collins about a mile away in the distance. Normally, I would have been romanced by this late-night snow scene in a new town, but I was tired, hungry and carrying a stuffed rucksack on an over-traveled back. So I walked towards a glowing gas station sign and when I arrived asked the kid behind the counter if there was a hostel in the town.

"Nope," the kid replied. "There ain't no youth hostel in Fort Collins. Shit, there's nothing in Fort Collins."

I was inclined to believe him. His hair was dyed orange, he wore baggy pants that showed off his spider-man boxer shorts, and had a thick silver wallet chain dangling down past his knees that probably weighed more than his skinny body. In other words, this kid had no reason to bullshit me, because if anyone could find something to do in a small rocky mountain town, it's a punk with an attitude.

Now I knew that Colorado State University was located in Fort Collins. So I asked the kid, "What do the college kids do here?" But that was a really stupid question, because they get drunk, smoke pot, and fuck, like every other college kid does, in every other college town in America, until they either enter the business world and die, or wake up and start living their own life.

"I guess if they're over 21, or got a fake ID, they go and drink at the bars," the kid answered. "Hell, I only took this job cuz I'm 18 and my fake got taken away. I work the graveyard shift here 'til 3:00 a.m., buy a few forties from my liberal boss, and then go hang out with my friends 'til dawn. Aside from that and snowboarding at nearby mountains, there 'aint shit to do," the kid restated.

"Do you have a phone book?" I asked him.

"Why?"

"Because I need to find a cheap hotel since this town doesn't have a hostel," I answered.

"Boulder has a hostel" the kid said.

"I know," I replied, "I once lived in that hostel for a month."

"I tell you what," the kid went on, "if you stick around here 'til three o'clock, when I get off, I'll give you a ride to Boulder.

"I appreciate the offer, but the hostel will be closed by then, and we'll both be sleeping on the street," I answered. "So can you call a cab for me?"

The kid called me a cab and I waited outside under the bright neon gas sign, trying to catch snowflakes on my tongue. When the cab pulled up, the kid walked outside and said to me, "Be here by noon tomorrow and I'll give ya a ride to Boulder."

I thanked him for his offer and told him I would sleep on it, and then I was off in a taxi driven by a young white guy with long curly orange hair who was wearing a Pink Floyd t-shirt. "Are there any cheap hotels in this town?" I asked him.

"There's nothing cheap downtown," he replied, "but there's some reasonable ones out on the interstate."

"I really don't want to stay in some chain joint out on the highway," I stated.

"Well there is a really cool old hotel that's probably been here ever since Fort Collins was settled," he suddenly remembered. "I think they rent rooms for pretty cheap sometimes if you get one without a bathroom. You know, it's like a European situation, the bathroom and showers are down the hall."

"That sounds good," I replied.

When the taxi dropped me off in front of the old hotel I couldn't help but sense that it had the historical demeanor of a journeyman's lodging, the kind of place that Jack London probably stayed at during his time up in the Yukon. I tried to open the front door, but it was locked so I rang the after hour's bell and within a few minutes a smiling middle-aged woman appeared and let me in saying, "It's blistery out there tonight young fella'. You should have called and warned me that you would be comin. I could have made you a nice cup of tea and turned the heat on in one of the rooms for you."

"That's okay," I replied. "I just need a simple room for the night where I can collect my thoughts and get some sleep."

"That I can do for you," she said, as she brought out a huge old guest register for me to enter my contact information in. When I finished supplying the pertinent details and paid the bill up front, she escorted me up an old staircase to a barren room along the very long and narrow second floor corridor. "You're the only guest tonight," she explained, "which means this place will be as quiet as a blanket of mountain snow."

There were well over a hundred rooms, and I knew this because I sauntered up and down the halls for a good hour like a wraith in search of someone to spook. Eventually, I went back to my room, turned the bedside lamp on and spent most of the night reading a book of short stories titled, "Christmas in the Heart," which my sister had sent to me while I was still living in Florida. She had heard of my plan to travel cross-country to work the season out in Colorado and sent me the nostalgic book with a brief note saying she would, "Miss you at Christmas little brother."

After reading several of the stories, I actually tried to call an old friend of mine down in Gainesville, Florida, but her roommate informed me in a rather annoyed tone, being that I had called at around five in the morning Gainesville time, that my friend had already left to spend the holidays with her family up north.

Here I was, alone in a strange room in Colorado reading sappy stories by very traditional mainstream writers who were pining and waxing poetic for love and connection at Christmas time. I put the book down for a moment and took stock of my trip: physically, I was very close to my supposed final destination of Winter Park; emotionally, spiritually, and psychologically however, I harbored no present intimacy towards the idea of going to work as a bartender at a ski lodge for the upcoming ski season. This left me with the inevitable question one asks oneself at three o'clock in the morning in an empty hotel just before Christmas: what was I doing out here?

In the morning, I walked across the street to a café that had a crackling fireplace in the center of the main room. I sat down at a small table by a window that looked out onto the main downtown pedestrian thoroughfare and ordered a mug of warm apple cider and French toast. As I waited for my breakfast, I spied the local residents streaming up and down the snowy street decked out in warm coats, hats, scarves, and mittens as they merrily hunted the local shops for last minute Christmas treasures. It was at this point of my journey, as I watched a young father pull his little boy down the block on a wooden sled, that I felt my heart open and began to realize where this road may be heading.

After a wonderful meal I walked back to the hotel, packed up my things, and went downstairs to the lobby to check the local bus schedule. I needed to catch a bus over to the gas station, where I could then hitch that ride to Boulder with the kid, but then I heard something that put a slight kink in my plan: "There ain't no buses that go over to that part a town. You're gonna have to call a cab," the girl at the front desk announced.

"Can you call me one?" I asked.

"Sure," she replied but then quickly stated that, "the taxi company said it's gonna take about an hour for them to get to ya."

"An hour?" I questioned. "But I've gotta meet my ride in fifteen minutes. Why is it gonna take an hour? It's eleven o'clock in Fort Collins, Colorado, for cryin out loud, how many people could there possibly be waiting for a taxi?"

"Not that many," the girl at the desk answered, "it's just that there's only two taxi services in this town, and one of them decided to take the day off for some reason."

"How far would it be for me to walk to the gas station from here?" I asked.

"I'd say about an hour with that pack you're luggin around and all the snow on the sidewalk," she answered.

I couldn't believe it. It was harder to get a taxi in Fort Collins than New York City. I decided to go outside and ask people on the street for a ride, after all, they all looked so cheery and full of holiday spirit. After about five minutes I had been turned down at least ten times. Then the girl from the front desk ran outside and yelled, "Rosita said she'll give you a ride, but you've got to hurry cuz she's leaving right away." I ran inside, threw my rucksack on and asked where Rosita was. "She's out back," the girl replied.

I kicked open the back door and ran out to the parking lot where I saw an old Mexican woman sitting in a beat-up blue pick-up truck listening to the Go-Go's. I'll never forget the song she was blasting either; it was "We got the Beat."

"Rosita?" I asked.

"Si," the woman responded. Then she motioned for me to jump into the back of the pick-up truck, which I did, and the moment I was safely lying down on my back, she pulled out of the parking lot and I waved goodbye to the old lonely Jack London hotel.

Within ten minutes we had arrived at the gas station where I jumped out of the back of the truck, yelled "Gracias" and "Hasta luego" to Rosita and then looked around for any sign of the kid. I quickly realized that he was not there, so I sat down against the cracked cement building, flipped up the collar on my coat, stuck my hands into my pockets and waited in the clear cold day.

I must have dozed off, because the next thing I knew a skinny figure stood over me saying, "Hey bro, wake up.

Let's get the hell outta this town and head on over to Boulder."

We loaded my gear into his car, an old metallic green Plymouth duster that had no passenger side window. "What happened to your window?" I asked.

"Who knows," the kid said, "it was there a few weeks ago, and then one day it was gone."

As we pulled out of the gas station parking lot and headed towards the highway, I took a second to say a prayer to bless all the drivers of all of the spontaneous rides that I had been given over the years of my nomadic living. I also sent a quick shout out to St. Patrick, the patron saint of bartenders, because if I had not picked up this skill set during my eighteenth year of life, I never would have ventured out to so many places and made the acquaintance of so many people during my time here.

"So what kind of music do you like?" the kid asked.

"I like just about everything," I responded.

"Except country?"

"That's correct," I said.

"You know I'm a songwriter," the kid boasted.

"Really?" I hinted.

"If you've got the time," the kid said, "we can swing by my house and pick up my guitar on our way to Boulder."

"I've got plenty of time," I replied, "and besides, I'd love to hear you play something."

A couple of minutes later we pulled off the highway and wound through a maze of side streets until we came to a stop in front of a trailer. "Why don't you come inside and have a drink," the kid offered.

"Sure," I replied.

The inside of the trailer was narrow and tight. There was a galley kitchen, his tiny bedroom, another bedroom and a cozy living room. "It ain't much, but it's all we got," he stated.

"Who do you live here with?" I asked.

"With my parents," the kid answered. "I know what you're thinkin, this is pretty close quarters for a young punk like me to live with his parents, but the truth of the matter is that they're my best friends."

"I wasn't thinking anything," I said to the kid, "but it is nice to hear someone your age talk so positively about your relationship with your parents."

"Well my parents are the ones who taught me how to play music. At night, if I'm not working at the gas station or out with my friends, we all sit around and jam together until one of us starts snoring. My dad's real good at making up lyrics, and my mom loves to shake the tambourine. I got nothin to complain about livin here with them, if you know what I mean" the kid said proudly.

"I think I do," I responded thoughtfully.

We talked for a little while longer while savoring the hoppy bite of two local microbrews, until eventually the kid grabbed his guitar and we headed back to the car.

"What do you wanna listen to on the way out to Boulder?" he asked.

"Well, besides the radio, what are my choices?" I inquired.

"I've got Tool, Weezer, Jane's Addiction…"

"Put Jane's in," I interrupted. "I could go for Perry right now."

"Me too," the kid agreed.

He popped the CD in and we cruised along the interstate at well over ninety miles per hour listening to one of America's most influential alternative rock bands. The moment was pure environmental adrenaline as we drove straight towards the heart of the Rockies while Perry Farrell yelled, "I was comin down the mountain."

When the song ended, the kid reached over and turned the volume all the way down. "You know," he began, "if you don't have anywhere to spend Christmas, you're more than welcome to join me and my parents at our home. My mom makes a pretty good turkey, and my dad is sure to whip up a bowl of his famous 7UP and cranberry punch."

As the freezing mountain wind flooded into the car through the non-existent passenger's side window, infiltrating every delicate exposed space between the buttons of my trusted sharp-shooters coat, I should have frozen in place like a stalactite hanging suspended in an underground cave. Yet I did not feel cold, because I now knew beyond the shadow of a doubt where this journey had always been leading me to.

"As much as I know spending Christmas with your family would be a truly wonderful experience," I explained, "I'm going to have to pass this time around. It's just that I've been on this road for a long time and I finally know where it's going, even if that's only for the next week or so."

"Where's that?" the kid asked.

"Home."

End of Judah
(San Francisco, California)

I walked into the café at the end of the N-Judah line and ordered a chai. It was tasteless, as most chai in San Francisco usually was. Even a large influx of honey wasn't enough to give the lackluster brew flavor.

I sat down on a couch, but then realized that it was in the sun, so I took my tea and walked over to another couch in a shady corner of the room. I sat next to a woman studying a medical textbook in her bare feet. I too slipped off my sandals and opened a book of Richard Brautigan's poetry. I guess she didn't like other people hanging their toes out, because she glanced at my bare appendages, packed up her stuff and moved on. Soon after, another soul walked through the sunlight and took her place.

"Hey brother," he said.

"What's up?" I responded.

"Oh, just another day, but I can't complain. Just happy to be alive," he said. "I damn near died this past year. Yup, I had cancer and it damned near killed me."

I looked at him. There were deep lines cut out under his eyes. His jaw looked like Patton's as a child, molded, but not completely formed. He had a slight mustache eddied with thin white and blonde hairs, and wore a black skull cap over his scalp, which had the beginnings of grey peach-fuzz sprouting.

"Lost it to chemo," he said, "but it's better than dyin. It's a miracle I'm alive. I had lymphoma, a real nasty disease, and if it wasn't for the chemo, all that radiation and lots of prayin, because I tell ya, I've never prayed so much in my whole life like I have over the last year, but I guess something heard me, and I'm still here. I'm still alive."

After he said the word alive, I heard music. It was the song, "Nothing Man," by Pearl Jam; the melody of the song wound around the man's torso like a divine snake. The lyrics described his very being.

"So where are you from?" he asked.

"I live in the Inner Sunset."

"No, I mean where were you born. Where'd you grow up?"

"Jersey," I answered.

"Jersey. I lived in Massachusetts for a while. I got kicked outta California for drugs. I knew everyone, all the people who did the drugs: The Dead, Jefferson Airplane, I partied with them all. Free love man, woo. Yeah, free love. Lotta my friends died on drugs. I knew Hendrix. Man that cat was a crazy great guitarist. My brother was the guitarist for Quicksilver. You heard a them?"

"No," I replied.

"They were good. I managed them. I was always around. Those were good times. But now's a good a time as any. I prayed a lot this year. The doctors though, they're the real saviors. This one lady doctor stayed with me throughout the whole thing and would always come in my room to check on me after chemo, cuz it drains ya. It's awful. I felt like dyin, felt like dyin so much I think I finally felt what livin must be like. No pain. Just some moments of no pain was livin to me."

In the distance a dim red sun was surrendering to the Pacific. The two people sitting on the sunny couch were talking on cell phones. A couple at a small table were calculating their credit card bills. A pair of high school kids were kissing on the loveseat.

"What do you do here?" he asked.

"I bartend at a restaurant, but I'm trying to be a writer," I informed him.

"I'm a writer," he said. "You wanna hear one of my poems?"

"Sure," I replied.

And then he proceeded to read from memory one of the most touching pieces I have ever heard. He kissed my soul with honesty, with love, with the knowledge that there are greater and lesser days still to come. Yet we face them all at this moment. He held my spirit in his air of acceptance and ushered me along to a peace I hadn't felt in some time. He wasn't a writer. He was a muse who had moved into the light-shadow of a human being.

We talked for a while longer, until I noticed the clock move and recognized a different song from the Pearl Jam album. I told him I needed to finish reading a book. He said, "Reading's important. You need to know things to get by in this world," and then thanked me for listening to him "babble away." He limped away slowly towards the door, turning around only once, to add, "It takes me a while."

Wandering towards Autumn in Southern Oregon
(San Francisco to Ashland)

One day in late September as I was walking through the Mission District of San Francisco on my way to work, the wind blew, and I smelled the scent of apples ripening on bountiful trees up in the Pacific Northwest. A sense of longing to be in cool fall weather up in the mountains where I could take part in the harvest and watch the leaves oxidize and turn wondrous shades of yellow, orange and red infused into me.

When I arrived at work, the place was already buzzing with hungry patrons. Later in the night, as the crowd died down and a sense of calm began to exist in the restaurant I asked around for people to cover my upcoming shifts. When I left work at a little after midnight, all of my shifts for the upcoming two weeks were covered. On my bus journey home from the trendy noisy Mission to the foggy and serene Cole Valley where I lived, I began to mentally pack my trusty worn rucksack.

In order to raise money for my harvest trip, I held a harvest dinner. I cooked a five-course supper for twelve people and served it in the formal dining room of the house where I was a boarder at the time. I decorated the table with leaves, pumpkins, squash, apples and autumnal flowers. All of the food and wine came from local organic farms. My friends and acquaintances placed their monetary donations in a hollowed out gourd that was passed around the table. That night I harvested enough money for a round-trip train ticket, food and two weeks of camping.

This trip had been building up within me for a while, so in the few days leading up to it I prepared myself by reading *Black Elk Speaks* and making a CD of my favorite songs by the band, *Explosions In The Sky*. I also asked my friend Jack if he would like to join me for the last weekend of the trip. He agreed to meet me there, basically wherever I ended up, because I had no idea where I was going.

I boarded the iron horse in Emeryville after a short bus trip from San Francisco, at about ten o'clock at night. The atmosphere outside the station was enchanted, as I waited to board the train where I would step back inside the mystery of travel. When the train arrived I walked onboard and headed upstairs where I placed my duffel bag and backpack on an empty aisle seat and settled in beside the window to watch the passing industrial parks until the buildings became sparse and the country opened up into flat stretches of farmland. The sky was clear and the moon seemed to follow the train until I fell asleep to dreams of marionberry pie and crisp fermented apple cider.

I awoke while it was still dark but could see bright dawn peak her head through the now diffused blanket of dim covering the earth. I got out my headphones and put in my new CD. The music began to play, fusing perfectly with the rising dawn illuminating the tall and erect soldier-like profiles of trees along the tracks. As we passed Mt. Shasta the song I was listening to built to a dramatic climax as the sun broke through the sky spotlighting its rays down upon the magnetic height of the mountain.

There is no amount of money that could buy from me the moment I spent on that train passing Mt. Shasta at dawn with my headphones on. I felt all the emotion of the previous year of learning, working, and healing in San Francisco break loose and go flooding through my body, releasing up and out into the aura of that illustrious mountain. I let the emotion flow from within me while outside my window Mt. Shasta emanated her golden glow. The other passengers began to stir as the cabin was saturated with morning light.

There is an intimacy that builds on a train between passengers after they have spent the night together stealing through small dusty towns and hinterlands known only to the hawks that hunt field mice among brushy midnight meadows. Upon waking you feel a comradeship with those who traverse the land in this slow time-honored way. A train is grounding. It allows you to slowly feel the length of the journey connecting to itself through winding track distance. Your consciousness is allowed to gradually adjust and expand with the land to the oncoming location.

The train pulled into Klamath Falls in mid-morning. A few of us got off and stretched our legs. The place was desolate save for one man standing next to a van.

"Do you want a lift on the Bend Express?" he asked.

"Sure," I replied.

One other guy agreed to a ride as well, so the three of us headed off together towards Bend. I had heard of Bend. I knew there was a hostel there that would probably have free beds this being midweek and all. The driver was a salmon fisherman and a salmon smoker. He gave both of his passengers a piece of salmon jerky. It was chewy, salty and made my mouth salivate. The driver told us that during the fishing season he and his sons catch a few hundred pounds of salmon and that income along with driving this shuttle sustains their family.

He dropped me off on a main road a little outside of downtown because the other passenger was in a rush to meet some people at a hunting lodge outside of Bend. I walked about a mile with my rucksack and duffel bag passing under a wonderful graffitied railroad trestle and eventually wound up at the hostel. It was a converted hotel, restaurant, microbrewery and hostel with colorful murals adorning the old memory-soaked wooden walls. I would be the only guest in the hostel tonight, a large space with twelve beds.

I wandered around Bend for a while and stopped at a microbrewery with an outside garden area. I chose a Porter to drink on this first day of my trip because I wanted that chocolate caramel chewiness to swirl around the inside of my mouth. As I sat and drank my beer, the sun began to show signs of waning. I finished my brew and journeyed a ways to one of the famous local buttes, basically a small dirt mountain, climbed up and looked out over the town of Bend situated smack dab in the Oregon high desert. From my vantage point I watched as the sky turned iridescent pink, orange, and then red.

The place I was staying at had an intimate bar hidden midst its lush garden area. There were a couple of small round tables situated around an old fireplace that sent warmth and red glow out into the tiny candlelit room. Earlier when I was walking around the town, I had gone into an esoteric bookshop and for some strange reason had noticed a flyer for a local girl who gave tarot card readings. I gave her a call from a pay phone and we agreed to meet at this magic little hideaway at the table closest to the fireplace.

When the Bend tarot reader arrived she was young, in her early twenties, and told me that she was a go-go dancer by trade who performed tarot readings, "Whenever spirit moved people to find her." She said that she loved doing tarot readings and only charged ten dollars for them, but didn't really like go-go dancing and was thinking about working at the local movie theatre instead. "But," she explained, "The money is much better at the club."

The few other patrons in the place were guys and they kept looking over at us. I guess they had never seen a tarot reading done at a bar before or maybe they were just checking out the lovely girl studying the cards. This reading was more obtuse than acute though. It gave me an overall view of what exactly my life was at that moment. What this trip was for me. It was a preparation, a ceremonial make ready that would infuse me with energy for more demanding situations later with regards to an ultimate distillation.

That's what I got out of it anyway. More than anything, she was entertaining and we both enjoyed participating in the ritual aspect of the reading. Then she left and I finished my malty slightly-hopped amber ale and headed back to fall asleep in my huge empty room, which little did I know was filled with dreams and omens.

That night I dreamt of a large white horse walking through a small field to a clear spring. The horse dipped his head down and drank of the water. There was steam rising from the pool. As I walked towards the edge of the field I came upon a place saturated with blackberry bushes. In front of me a small mountain path ascended in switchbacks. The horse looked back at me and walked up the mountain trail. Then I woke up.

In the morning I took a stroll around the downtown and decided to leave. My night had been fruitful, but my intuition said to move on. The bus station was about a mile away and took me about twenty minutes to walk over there with my bag slung on my back. Upon arrival I perused the schedules and bought a ticket to Salem. This journey would take me over and through the mountains to the eastern side of Oregon. Once in Salem I would transfer from my small bus to a larger one heading down towards Medford and Southern Oregon.

Fate and luck were on my side as there was only one other passenger on the short bus. I stretched out across the seats and gazed out the window in awe as we rolled through little forest hamlets and then up and over and down the mountains again. At one point I thought I saw two hawks waltzing in the sky.

When we arrived in the capital city of Salem the bus station was fairly empty. I had an hour to pass so I strolled around the quaint downtown, where I bought a loaf of fresh baked bread and sat down and ate it in a park along the Willamette River. I remembered that my Athens, Georgia, poetess comrade Chloe had spent one year in Salem living with her aunt and uncle. She had liked it but eventually grew tired of all the rain.

The bus from Salem to Medford was packed with people going down to San Francisco and Los Angeles. When we stopped for a short break in the college town of Eugene the bus station was filled with drifters: young kids with bandanas and rucksacks and older guys with thermoses of booze and stained flannel shirts stashed in goodwill duffels. I was drifting as well, so I boarded the bus, settled in, sat back, looked out the window and listened to the banter. *What stories we drifters can tell.* There was no need for my headphones on this leg of the trip, as I had all the entertainment I needed.

There was one kid out of all the crazy passengers on the bus that will always stick with me. He was a big tall kid that kind of resembled the character of "Chief" from the movie *One Flew over the Cuckoo's Nest; a* slow-witted honest forthright soul who would never hurt a fly. He kept telling me that his mother, who was a very spiritual Native American woman, had sent him on this trip that had originated all the way up in Spokane, Washington, and would eventually end near Flagstaff, Arizona, where his grandmother lived. His mother believed that his life force was being sucked out of him up in Spokane and that the mountains outside of Flagstaff, where she had been raised, would reenergize him and usher him towards manhood and his true destiny in this world.

The bus pulled into Medford at a little after nine o'clock at night. I walked off the streamlined silver vessel and grabbed my rucksack from the underneath compartment. Then I looked out into the street and was just about to sit down against an old brick building and ponder my situation in the fresh moonlight when a very pretty young girl asked me, "Well, what are you going to do now?"

"Are you talking to me?" I asked her.

"You're the one looking quite perplexed with what to do next," she replied.

Not only was this girl attractive, she was intelligent and had a sarcastic sense of humor. As a Jersey boy, I appreciated that. "I hadn't figured that out yet," I answered.

"Well," she replied, "I came here to collect my sister and now I am heading into Ashland. Would you like to go there?"

Ashland? My friend Michael Murphy had told me that he had once come across this town on a trip up to Seattle from San Francisco. He told me it was quite charming and had a nice downtown. I thought to myself for a second and then proclaimed, "Yes, I would like to go to Ashland."

"That's good, because that's where we're going."

The girl drove an old beat-up small blue car that had stuffing spilling out of the front seats and no seat belts. However it was a ride with two young pretty girls who had nomadic souls like mine so I sat back and enjoyed the ride. The girl driving was the older sister of the girl riding in the back. The girl driving lived in Ashland. The girl riding in the back had just moved here from the mountains of

Tennessee to live with her big sister. Where were their parents? Who knows? They were here, giving me a lift.

"So where do you want to go in Ashland?" the girl driving asked.

"I don't know. Are there any hot springs there?"

"You're joking right?" she responded.

"Why?" I asked.

"Because there's a great place right outside of town where I actually used to live for a while and you can camp there or stay in a tee-pee if you like. It's a special place to be," she replied.

"How could I not stay there after that introduction," I answered.

We drove towards the springs and I could feel my body becoming loose with the anticipation of a morning soak. In a short time we arrived. The girl driving gave me a hug and said, "Be sure to soak it all in. And in the morning, when you wake up, go and pick some blackberries for breakfast, there are tons of them out in the back of the property by the hills."

I promised to find the blackberries and then slapped her kid sister who was lounging in the backseat a high five and they were off and I had arrived. I took a deep breath and inhaled the smell of minerals in the air.

I walked into the office as it was about to close and the woman seated at the front desk rented me a tee-pee for the next ten days. The price was reasonable and included use of the springs, dry sauna, natural showers and locker room inside the compound.

As I walked across the property to my lodging, I looked up at the moon and the stars, natural wonders that I hardly ever saw in San Francisco. They were bedazzling in their clarity and luminescence, they seemed so close and intelligent. The moon was heavy and orange-tinted. The harvest was approaching. I could sense the apples vibrating on the trees.

The tee-pee was fairly large in diameter and very tall with an opening at the top that could be adjusted with two long poles. There was a deep fire pit dug in the center of the cylindrical space. I took my sleeping bag out of my duffel bag and placed a rolled up sweatshirt at the bag's opening for a pillow. I retrieved a small flashlight from my rucksack and headed out to scrounge up enough firewood to get me through what had become a very chilly Oregon autumn night.

Gathering firewood proved easier than I thought and within about an hour I had a vibrant fire whose silhouetted flames danced magically along the stretched canvas of the tee-pee. I took out a bundle of sage that I had bought at a farmers market in San Francisco and threw it onto the flames. The medicinal white smoke smudged through me, cleansing all of the conversations and transient energies I had been exposed to on the bus trip out of my psyche, allowing me to be present with the physical and spiritual heat of the fire and the sublime beauty of smoke filtering out of the small hole at the top of my cone shaped lodging.

The smoke was the essence of the burning wood releasing up and back out into the wilderness. It was a very deep natural blessing bestowed upon me. A beautiful chain of events that led me exactly where I wanted to be---cozy by the fire in the fall up in Oregon.

After a blissful sleep I woke up and started a fire in order to boil some water for tea and keep me warm when I came back from my morning soak. Back in San Francisco I had blended a male tonic tea for myself: fennel seeds, cinnamon bark, sarsaparilla root and saw palmetto berries. I tossed my earthy mixture into the small pot of bubbling liquid to let it steep and then observed the flames of the campfire while seated on a little bench I had made from a wooden plank and two cinder blocks, which I had found the previous night while collecting firewood.

While waiting for the tea water to become infused, I remembered what the girl who had given me a ride to the springs had said about there being blackberries budding on the back of the property, so I made my way out of the tee-pee and walked west as the dazzling morning light warmed the back of my neck.

Within a short time I came to a cluster of blackberry bramble growing along a small service road. There were tons of the tiny dark purple jewels clinging to the bushes. I plucked one from its origin and placed it in my mouth. I let the berry sit there, feeling its shape, texture, allowing its color to saturate my tongue. Then I bit into its luscious dark body, which burst all over my taste buds, presenting my senses with a rush of tart and sweet.

All of a sudden I remembered the dream I had at the hostel in Bend of the white horse dipping his head into the steaming springs to drink and then heading off up into a small switchback trail by a row of blackberry bushes. I looked around me. I was there. It all made sense. All of it. Life. The journey. Arrival. What departure really is to someone presently on their path. Pilgrimage. Travel. Movement. Stillness. Roots. Contemplation. Fruit. Harvest. Autumn. The Fall.

I spent the next five days wandering around the small hills, soaking in the spring waters, hitch-hiking into the quaint downtown, eating marionberry pies, drinking soft and hard apple ciders, writing poetry, harvesting fruit, and partaking in various seasonal festivals and gatherings with the locals.

Then my friend Jack arrived on his motorcycle after making the long haul from San Francisco up I-5, harboring a bottle of homemade absinthe his girlfriend had made on an herb farm in Sebastopol. After a soak and some blackberries, we built a roaring fire and ritualistically consumed the absinthe in our tee-pee from midnight into the wee hours of the morning as our inebriated minds stalked the smoke from the fire as it journeyed up and out of the planted canvas shelter into the great holy hole of sky and universe wrapping our bodies like a blanket inside this earthly dream of organic mystery and its individual incantations of wholeness and wonder.

Darlene's Garden
(Cortes Island, British Columbia)

I had always lived very austerely with regards to money and possessions, but in November of 2006 I received a distinct interior message to further explore the nature of my relationship to the ever-evolving creation without the burdens that money and the expectation of certain wages can place upon one's service to the world. Thus I decided to embark on a two year-long odyssey of what Hindus refer to as karma yoga, or what Christians would deem service to my fellow brothers and sisters.

This journey took me back out to the West Coast and then on up into the Evergreen territory of the Pacific Northwest. It was while working as a gardener at an artistic retreat center in the Northeast when I first heard the name, Cortes Island. When my work at the arts place was finished, I made a brief visit to San Francisco to visit a loved one and then I embarked on a long and thought-provoking journey to Cortes Island that involved a cheap plane ride from Oakland to Seattle, a bus from Seattle to Vancouver, and then hitching a car ride from Vancouver to Campbell River, followed by two ferry passages until I ultimately reached my destination.

On this small island nestled in-between mainland British Columbia and Vancouver Island, I would be volunteering my services to the karma yoga program at a prominent spiritual retreat center. The majority of my work would be with helping to maintain the beautiful gardens and cleaning the guest rooms.

It was during this time that I met a local girl named Kelsey, who lived with her mother on a piece of land near Smelt Bay. Over time Kelsey and I became friends until one night after work she invited me to her mother's house to enjoy a gin and tonic on their peaceful deck. The funny thing was that the second I stepped onto that property, I felt a deep sense of connection to place like I had only felt a few other times in my life before.

This was a definite sign for me because I have always had a deep interest in how places and people can come together in seamless unity at certain times when the universe is perfectly aligned, or in other words, the path has been intuitively followed by the wayfarer.

Months earlier, while living and working in the countryside up in the Northeast, I had experienced a vision of a piece of land near the sea: it contained a small apple orchard and was surrounded by a ring of tall fir trees. In that vision I was told to "come and tend to the land so that those who lived upon it may be healed by its bounty." It was a clear call to service that had planted itself deep within me. As I sat on the porch drinking a gin

and tonic with Kelsey, her mother pulled up in a beat-up black pick-up truck. When she walked onto the porch and looked at me I felt a natural kinship with her.

Her name was Darlene, but she had recently changed her name to "Dhar" to reclaim a sense of personal power after a wounding divorce that took her away from the family home on a neighboring island. After going inside to clean herself up a bit, as she had just come home from working the night shift at the local organic food co-op, Dhar welcomed me to her home by clinking my glass with her own gin and tonic and then handing me a big bag of organic potato chips.

Dhar said that the potato chips were a gift and I could eat them all because she was consuming only raw food. She was convinced that eating a raw diet was a way to attain higher consciousness. Over the course of the next hour Dhar told me about her beliefs in numerology, astrology, shamans, and when I went to use the bathroom I found an extensive New Age library with every kind of channeling and esoteric text arranged on numerous bookshelves together with crystals, dream-catchers and tarot decks. Dhar was lost and searching for answers everywhere but inside of her authentic self. As I stood there, I suddenly remembered a very powerful dream I had experienced a week before in San Francisco:

> *I was standing in a parking lot next to a pick-up truck when two people on bicycles pulled up to me and said, "Let's go." I looked into the truck and saw a small child sitting there. The child looked at me and I looked at him and then with a sense of overwhelming love and release I replied to the two cyclists, "Okay."*
>
> *A bike appeared for me and suddenly we were pedaling down a highway that quickly turned into a dirt road. The dirt road led into a swampy forest where we eventually came to a rustic camp. At this*

camp we were taught how to shoot a bow and arrow and then the cyclists, who before this point had been kind of amorphous, turned into a tall thin wizard-like middle-aged man with tattoos and a dark demeanor and a younger shy but pretty woman who seemed to be caught up in his magical spell.

We were all sitting together on a small atoll in the middle of a swamp when the wizard fell asleep and I beckoned to the younger woman to get up and come with me. As I walked toward the edge of the atoll a small bridge appeared and I crossed onto dry land. However, the young woman in her attempt to extricate herself from the sleeping grasp of her master had awoken him and he looked directly at me and then said something aloud that I could not understand.

It was at this point that I saw a very large alligator climb out of the swamp near to where I was standing and stare at me menacingly. I began to run and the alligator burst off in my direction. After a few moments I turned to see the beast right behind me and then as I looked forward again two vile-looking black hounds with spit and foam frothing from their snarling mouths were sprinting directly at me from the other direction. When the hounds got within a few feet of me they leapt into the air with their biting jowls showing off rows of jagged sinister teeth, and as I closed my eyes and awaited the inevitable thrashing I stood transfixed in that moment with the most glorious feeling of peace that had ever come upon me.

Eventually I turned around and found that the dogs were sitting calmly next to the now peaceful corpse of the alligator. Then I lay on the ground and looked up at what had transformed into a night sky

where a beautiful circle of spirits seemed to be
waltzing together in a circular pattern that somehow
seemed to tell me that I was safe, and among my
cosmic family.

When I walked back outside and took my place on the deck beside Dhar and Kelsey, I gazed at the wonderful property lined with tall fir trees while listening to Dhar proclaim, "And there's a small apple orchard in the back of the property." I knew that I was home; that the vision that had been revealed to me that winter night many months ago in the frosty countryside had become my present reality. Furthermore, the mystical dream in the swamp was a sign that any transgressions from my past had been absolved, and that here on this land, if I surrendered my will to stewardship and community, I would be shown the way to create healing.

As the three of us sat there on the deck I looked deeply into Dhar and could sense her pain but also her buried luminous heart. It was the same aching that I would come to see in so many beautiful souls who lived on that remote island: the pain of separation from self, which had been caused by the combination of some kind of familial or social life trauma and/or the heartless dogma of fundamental Christianity, leading them to leave mainstream society and the church to seek solace in the ungrounded methods and trendy communal currents of New Age spirituality.

I said to Dhar, "I noticed that you have Juliano's cookbook, *RAW*. I worked for him at his first little restaurant in San Francisco back when raw food wasn't so trendy."

"Wow, that's amazing," she responded.

"But one thing that I always keep in mind as someone who travels a lot and is often invited to take part in meals in other people's homes is something that Jesus is credited with saying, "There is nothing outside a man which by going into him can defile him; but the things which come out of a man are what defile him." To which I then added, "After all of my studies and personal experiments with regards to food and human consciousness over the last ten years, the one thing I can relate to you is that food prepared with love is the best thing for us, and it tastes better too."

At this point I held up the bag of potato chips and tore it open like it was the holy bread of Christ. It was then that I noticed a humungous black cat run up the stairs of the deck, sit down right in front of me and then look up into my eyes as if to telepathically say, "This is it pal, give me a chip and we're buds for life, tell me to scram and you'll regret it." I put a chip on the ground next to the behemoth, and he calmly licked the salt off of it and then broke it into little pieces with his gigantic paws so he could casually partake of it bit by bit.

"That's Claus," Kelsey stated. "You know like Santa Claus."

"But he's usually not as jolly as Santa, yet he seems to like you a lot dude," Dhar exclaimed.

"I'm a dog person myself," I said. "But this guy looks more like a short squatty puma than a house cat. What did you say this cat's name was?"

"Claus," Kelsey replied.

I looked at the cat. He looked at me. "Nope," I stated. "His name isn't Claus. It's H.S. Gargantuan."

"What's the H.S. stand for?" Kelsey asked.

"It stands for the first thought I had when I saw that big guy run up onto the deck and ask me for a chip, "Holy Shit," I replied.

We all laughed and only stopped when Dhar decreed, "Hey dude, pass the chips."

Kelsey looked at her mother with a puzzled expression and inquired, "I thought that you were only eating raw food mom?"

"I thought I was too," Dhar answered. "But right now I feel like those potato chips are as healthy as wheatgrass, and they taste a whole lot better."

Then it happened: Dhar looked over at Kelsey, Kelsey looked over at Dhar, and then Dhar looked over at me and with a big grin on her face she asked, "So when are you moving here dude?"

The next day I pitched a tent alongside a wooden fence on the Western edge of Dhar's property. It was the beginning of July and I would stay and work the land with Dhar until November. The following spring I returned in the beginning of May and stayed until the end of the autumn harvest in October when my work with the land and Dhar was complete.

The seeds of what we planted and harvested together during our time as "Orchard Family" on that beautiful *terroir* up the hill from Smelt Bay, continue to grow and blossom within me.

~Fin~